**AD** Architectural Design

# Fame + Architecture

Guest-edited by Julia Chance
and Torsten Schmiedeknecht

**WILEY-ACADEMY**

## Architectural Design
### Vol 71 No 6 November 2001

ISBN 0-470-84229-6
Profile No 154

**Editorial Offices**
International House
Ealing Broadway Centre
London W5 5DB
T: +44 (0)20 8326 3800
F: +44 (0)20 8326 3801
E: info@wiley.co.uk

**Editor**
Helen Castle

**Executive Editor**
Maggie Toy

**Production**
Famida Rasheed

**Art Director**
Christian Küsters ↘ CHK Design

**Designer**
Owen Peyton Jones ↘ CHK Design

**Picture Editor**
Famida Rasheed

**Advertisement Sales**
01243 843272

# For Henri

**Photo Credits**
Δ Architectural Design

Abbreviated positions
b=bottom, c=centre, l=left, r=right, t=top

p 4 courtesy Diller + Scofidio, photo: Michael Moran; pp 6-7 photo: © Timothy Greenfield-Sanders; pp 12 & 13 © OMA; p 16 photo © Charles Jencks; p 17 © Squire Haskins as featured in the book Kings of Infinite Space by Charles Jencks, Academy Editions, 1983, the publishers have made every attempt to contact the copyright holder; pp 18, 20-22 RIBA Library Photographs Collection; p 24 (far bl) & p 32 courtesy Foster and Partners, photo: © Ian Lambot; p 24 (bl) courtesy Foster and Partners, photo: © James H Morris; p 24 (br) courtesy Foster and Partners, photo: © John Linden: p 24 far (br), p 25 (t & far bl), p 27-8 & p 32 courtesy Foster and Partners, photos: © Nigel Young/Foster and Partners; p 25 (bl to br) & p 29 courtesy Foster and Partners, photos: © Richard Davies; p 26 (b) courtesy Foster and Partners, photo: © Tim Street-Porter; p 30 (l) courtesy Foster and Partners, photo: © Ken Kirkwood; p 30 (r) courtesy Foster and Partners, photo: © John Donat; p 31 & 33 courtesy Charles Jencks; pp 34, 35 & 37 © Sean Griffiths; p 36 (l) © Sean Griffiths, photo: Andy Keate; p 36 (r) courtesy Kesselskramer; p 38 courtesy The Architects Journal, photo: John Stillwell; p 39 courtesy The Architects Journal, photo: Morley von Sternberg; p 40 courtesy The Architects Journal, photo: Cliff Bawden; p 42 © David Banks/Country Life Picture Library; pp 43-7 © John Outram; pp 50-52 photos: © Torsten Schmiedeknecht; p 54 (r) © Herz/Poeting; pp 58-9 & 61-2(b) © Diller + Scofidio; p 59 (r) courtesy Diller + Scofidio, photo: Marc LaRosa; pp 60 (t & bl), 62(t) & 63 courtesy Diller + Scofidio photo: Michael Moran; p 60 (br) courtesy Diller + Scofidio, photo: Imanishi; p 64 (t) © Phyllis Lambert Archive. Collection Centre Canadien d'Architecture / Canadian Centre for Architecture; p 64 (b) Collection Centre Canadien d'Architecture/Canadian Centre for Architecture, Montréal Ezra Stoller © Esto; p 65 (t) Collection Centre Canadien d'Architecture/Canadian Centre for Architecture, Montréal © Richard Pare; p 65 (b) Collection Centre Canadien d'Architecture / Canadian Centre for Architecture, Montréal © Lohan Associates/CCA; pp 66-70 photos: © Julie Cook; pp 71-4 photos: © Jonathan Harris; p 75 photo: Julian Broad

© Vogue/The Condé Nast Publications Ltd; pp 85-9 photos: © Julius Shulman; p 90 RIBA Library Photographs Collection; pp 91-4 courtesy Howard Martin

Δ Architectural Design +
pp 96+ & 98+ © Duccio Malagamba-fotografía de arquitectura; pp 97+, 98(b)-100+ courtesy Alvaro Siza; p 101(t)+ photo: © David Joseph; pp 101(b)+ ,p104+, p102 (r)+, p105 (t)+ & 106-7+ courtesy SHoP Sharples Holden Pasquarelli; p 102(l)+ photo: © Karen Ludlam; p 105(b)+ photo: © Eileen Costa; pp 110-1+ © Gans & Jelacic.

In memory of Royston Landau who passed away shortly before publication.

Cover image
Christian Küsters ↘ CHK Design
Timepix/Time Magazine/Rex

**Subscription Offices UK**
John Wiley & Sons Ltd.
Journals Administration Department
1 Oldlands Way, Bognor Regis
West Sussex, PO22 9SA
T: +44 (0)1243 843272
F: +44 (0)1243 843232
E: cs-journals@wiley.co.uk

**Subscription Offices USA and Canada**
John Wiley & Sons Ltd.
Journals Administration Department
605 Third Avenue
New York, NY 10158
T: +1 212 850 6645
F: +1 212 850 6021
E: subinfo@wiley.com

**Annual Subscription Rates 2001**
Institutional Rate: UK £150
Personal Rate: UK £97
Student Rate: UK £70
Institutional Rate: US $225
Personal Rate: US $145
Student Rate: US $105

Δ is published bi-monthly.
Prices are for six issues and include postage and handling charges. Periodicals postage paid at Jamaica, NY 11431. Air freight and mailing in the USA by Publications Expediting Services Inc, 200 Meacham Avenue, Elmont, NY 11003

Single Issues UK: £19.99
Single Issues outside UK: US $32.50
Order two or more titles and postage is free. For orders of one title add £2.00/US $5.00. To receive order by air please add £5.50/US $10.00

**Postmaster**
Send address changes to Δ Publications Expediting Services, 200 Meacham Avenue, Elmont, NY 11003

Printed in Italy. All prices are subject to change without notice.
[ISSN: 0003-8504]

# Fame + Architecture

## Guest-edited by Julia Chance and Torsten Schmiedeknecht

∆D

Infamy, celebrity, publicity, marketing, identity, viability, recognition, renown, perpetuity. Fame is many different things to many different people. For any architect the establishment of a name or reputation, even at a local level, is a fundamental necessity. It is a prerequisite to client confidence and gaining vital commissions. Recognition within the architectural community pulls practices out of obscurity on to competition shortlists and into invited competitions. Substantial fame propels architects into another public orbit – on to the cover of Time magazine, making them the subjects of major art retrospectives. On reaching the heady heights of Frank Gehry, Lord Foster or Daniel Libeskind, architects are transformed into household names that in the media become the face of contemporary architecture. The payback for the members of this exclusive league is their qualification for the top architectural jobs – the opportunity to build great and iconic buildings and bid for enduring architectural fame. For as Julia Chance and Torsten Schmiedeknecht have succeeded in demonstrating in this issue, fame is not a mere bonfire of vanities but a real and dynamic force within architectural practice. △ *Helen Castle*

*Julia Chance and Torsten Schmiedeknecht*

At a party a couple of years ago a young architect responded to the question, 'And how´s work going?' with the statement: 'We´ve got a few projects on; some quite nice work really. Not all of it will be publishable but you might be able to find some in the odd magazine soon.'

He had just set up on his own after having worked for five years with a renowned practice and the conversation took place at a Christmas event full of aspiring fellow architects, whose general aim, it transpired, was to have their projects published. The conversations were not about the architectural qualities of the projects, or their experiences of working them, but about the possibility that they would appear in print when they were completed.

The architectural press offers a kind of acknowledgement for the efforts of the architect. But the yearning for such acknowledgement has led to a situation where the press now occupies the role of an authority that judges the quality of the architectural work, in terms of whether it is suitable for publishing or not. Architects now look to those who publish in the way that students look to tutors – *for an authoritative acknowledgement of what is good.* In this scenario there is little or no concern for the critical context of the published work.

Architecture is currently experienced more than ever in a mediated way through television, film, the Internet and print media. There have never been more publications celebrating and promoting the work of architects within society and the number is increasing. Architecture and its reproduction, it seems, has become a specialised discipline, mostly catering for itself, and an architect's existence is often only seriously acknowledged after an initial baptism of his or her work in print.

Through its own services the press reaffirms its own importance: a job recently advertised in *Building Design* stated that the candidate would be 'working on good projects which are likely to be published'.

Perhaps part of the reason for the yearning for publicity is the difficulty of assessing real architectural quality, and also the length of time it takes to test whether a work endures. These factors create a void within the hectic pace of day-to-day architectural practice, and the immediate gratification of seeing a completed project printed in a magazine offers reassurance along the way that the considerable effort involved in completing architectural projects is worthwhile.

It was in the aftermath of the party mentioned above that we started to think about the relationship between the production of architecture and the ways in which the work and the architect are acknowledged in the broader social realm. Our first reaction was to be somewhat critical of the way in which architects described projects in terms of their potential publishability with no apparent concern for a level of criticism of the work, or its context. To us, the fact that a project was published did not necessarily mean that it was interesting or good. However, it is not possible to ignore the significance of the mass-mediated image in terms of the dissemination of ideas and the general development of architectural discourse.

Our interest in the desire architects have to see their work published, and the reasons behind this phenomenon, soon developed into an interest in the more historically consistent desire that members of the profession have shown for their work and themselves to be noticed generally, in many cases with the ultimate if unpublicised aim of becoming famous.

Although architects freely display their desire to be published they will rarely admit that they deliberately pursue fame. There is a strong element of the taboo in the realm of self-publicity and architecture, with many things that no one wants to be seen to be orchestrating. There is a desire to be acknowledged without being seen to desire acknowledgement.

Our investigations led to more fundamental questions, such as who becomes famous and how? In this issue of *Architectural Design* we investigate the relationships that exist between fame and architecture and in order to do so we incorporate the thoughts of a wide spectrum of architects and thinkers. We take the opportunity here to say 'thank you' to them, for helping us to begin to find out about a realm that we find interesting; and also to thank the publishers, Wiley, for giving us the opportunity to enjoy for ourselves the feeling that comes from seeing one's name in print and allowing us to participate in that age-old game of becoming conspicuous … Δ *Julia Chance and Torsten Schmiedeknecht*

Opposite
Dining Room in Diller +
Scofidio's Brasserie in
the Seagram Building.

Some Though
the Institutior

s on Fame and
of Architecture

David Dunster sheds light on the phenomenon of fame by delving into the conundrum of what architecture is. He explains how for architects press attention is not a mere add-on, but endemic and immanent to their continued existence – 'publish, exhibit, network' being the 'verbs leading to building'.

If only someone could convincingly and concisely define architecture, or even an architect, then what happens in architecture and to architects would cease to cause anguish. Because architects handle large amounts of other people's money, their position in law keeps them on the borders of that wild area inhabited by the Finer Arts. Defining architecture as what architects do is about as convincing as defining eggs as what chickens do. The solipsism hides many paradoxes. Without definition, time and history evaporate leaving the uncomfortable residue that suggests that what any lowly paid architectural assistant does tomorrow is equal to what architectural names from the past did. Borromini surely sharpened his pencil, but never issued architectural variation orders. Nor did he get to be an architect in Rome in the 17th century through a state-controlled system of education, neither did he read with glee about Bernini's travails through a weekly professional newspaper. What has evolved since Borromini practiced is something like an architectural system, which obeys laws specific to itself, for intending architects to succeed in their avocation through a particular and demanding process which uses an argot in which words are used in ways peculiar to architects. There are even mechanisms for reinforcing architects in their belief that they are architects. Architecture defines architects by virtue of having evolved into an institution. The institution architecture, not to be confused with an institute, comprises all the mechanisms by which architects reproduce architects.

Consider tomorrow without architects – how could the institution be abolished? Firstly, assuming there was still some unexpressed need in society for architects to do architecture, abolishing the title in one country would merely mean that architects from others would step in to the vacated role – if that were not taken over by other people who just felt like taking the title. Secondly, it would take a lifetime for those in education to die off, shades of the Jedi knights; and thirdly, abolishing architects might just make them very popular with any group that was opposed to the forces that abolished them. By characterising Architecture as an institution – I will use a capital A for Architecture in this context – we can see why its future is so intricately bound up with the conditions of the profession's current structures.

Architects are now produced for society through an educational process equal to that of other professions. While enduring this process, aspirants are gradually exposed to more and more of the work and uncertainties of their chosen career, and those who qualify are enjoined to undertake more education through continuous professional development courses to add to their skills, knowledge, professionalism and ability to stay *au courant*. In education, the state of the art is reinforced by the teaching process, reined in by criteria pronounced current by the profession but invariably, and perhaps inevitably, out of date as soon as a pronouncement is made. Once qualified as far as higher education is concerned, the architect as a member of the profession takes on a publicly mandated role to further filter entry to it. Once admitted to the profession, the architect's job of doing architecture should be, and sometimes is, supported by minimal indicators of performance. Increasingly, media attention reinforces discussion of this entire apparatus of education and induction. The attention comes not only from media specifically for architects, through journals and professional meetings, but also from newspapers, radio and television. Reinforcing architects' sense of their own right to exist, the media therefore play a crucial role in perpetuating the institution Architecture, and contribute to Architecture's very claim to be an institution. Press attention is not an add-on, but is endemic and immanent to architecture's continued existence. Without magazines and media attention architecture would go the way of anthropology.

As politics, economics and society struggle to become more transparent to more and more people, so the results of this aim for transparency throughout all institutions have brought a greater exchange of information about Architecture, both within and outside the institution. Including lay members on any kind of architectural panel makes the rash assumption that they can penetrate the private language architects use, but signifies that the public nature of what architecture happens to be has to have substance. If Architecture is as imbricated with itself as I am suggesting, change in any part of the institution will result in changes in the other parts. Publicity (is there a bad kind?) affects the processes of education, the mechanisms of regulation and the way in which the profession sees itself. Publicity deals with what is news, and for the arts this means what is new. The lone practitioner doing a decent job cannot hope to be published, but could not even get to do a decent job if there were no publicity for those who do a newsworthy one. Asking who controls the publicity raises yet another spectre of more institutions – the fourth estate and its electronic bigger brother – who, just like architecture, have their own networks, internal structures and rules of engagement. This is the fact that some architects understand while others wish it would go away. The basic rule of publicity is reliability. Fail to deliver on one occasion and you are off the list. A television programme goes out once and if you can't make it to the studio it will not be rescheduled. Turn up on a bad one-liner day and you won't be asked back either. These little rules do not necessarily hold in architectural practice.

The media then makes demands; it is a monster hungry for news, sound bites, novelty. Arguments which have been cogently made for architecture to become normative, quiet, good-mannered and temperate fail in this arena unless they are pronounced by a personage from a higher-level institution than architecture. They cannot produce the novelty, are not so designed and become another nail in the coffin of good practice. Television and, increasingly, the press want razzle-dazzle, the familiar shock of the new and something photogenic, so forget complicated sections. The blood stream into which architecture has to be injected does not run on a common element like oxygen, but upon the exceptional and rare. Art practice measures up to the media's demands rather better than architecture. Moreover, the media requires stars and will create them if it has to. Hardly a weekend goes by without a long press interview with a newish actor – not a director or, perish the thought, a writing

hack but someone who is photogenic and just enough like an everyday Joe to offer surfaces which the average reader (who's she?) can identify with. Architects need not worry about their hair; in general they can fall into the category of *joli laid*.

To waylay the monster media, architects frequently hold the mirror to fashion. If architecture becomes merely a branch of that industry, the ephemerality of mode will erode all thought of eternal truths. The familiar mysteries give way to the unknown. Architecture is lost. Consider this passage from *The New Yorker*:

> In all fields where art meets commerce – fashion, publishing, entertainment, the art world, the music business – a system must be in place whereby talented people become known to those with influence, receive their backing and are brought before the public. To those labouring in obscurity, these systems appear to be deeply flawed. But, as anyone who has ever worked in a publishing house reading the slush pile can attest, virtually every genius that can be discovered is discovered. There is a simple economic reason for that: just as chemical companies need new compounds, retailers and galleries and movie studios need new stars so they devote themselves to research and development. By this time, the cultural nervous system has become so extensive and so acute that the cortex in New York will register stimuli as far away as, say, Dallas Texas, the native homeland of Erykah Badu.[1]

The author of this recognises that even in ephemera there is a system whose mysterious workings are concealed behind a sleek surface of apparent common sense, one so sleek that it can even dispose of the undiscovered. The antennae belong to those who both move and shake to make names, and whose fame

In the recent 20th century three figures stand out as masterful in media terms. First, Frank Lloyd Wright, then Le Corbusier and, still with us, Philip Johnson.

depends upon their ability to find the future famous. In the past they were hostesses or impresarios. That earlier age would recognise the system's function as one of finding favour or, more acceptable, seeking patronage for its protégés. In either Stalin's Russia or Blair's Britain exercising the power of patronage escapes ideological critique since the great and the good will always decide for the best possible reasons. These reasons do change over time. But we can recognise the architectural profession's deepest fears in this quotation from the weekly guide to the opinion capital of the world.

In the recent 20th century three figures stand out as masterful in media terms. First, Frank Lloyd Wright, then Le Corbusier and, still with us, Philip Johnson. Wright loved the press, and the press loved his gimcrack, cracker-barrel style. Ever ready with a *bon mot* for all occasions, he capitalised on uniting two American fantasies: the fix-it inventor and the genius of the soil. Better yet, he knew how to dress for photography. Le Corbusier on the other hand, being a Swiss émigré, was more Parisian than the real article. He played the bohemian intellectual with style, knew how to doctor his publications and had a way with words. His comment to journalists when he arrived in New York, that the skyscrapers were too short, guaranteed attendance at his lectures. Knowing how to be outrageous, and polite, meant he could get away with proposing his standard urban solution on every city he visited. Drawings made over dinner in Chicago in 1935 could be resited almost anywhere.[2]

Philip Johnson, however, made it – as Le Corbusier did and Wright did – on to the Leslie Martin he purred that he, Johnson, was surely the better architect. As ringmaster of Manhattan and patron of the controllable avant-garde, Johnson exercises such power over the media that only Michael Sorkin is on record in critical vein. A recent photograph taken at the Century Club showed enough architects who should know better (including Zaha Hadid and Rem Koolhaas) crowded around the nonagenarian in adulation.[4] No doubt the conversation sparkled, but it is a pity about the architecture.

Fame cuts across the categories of architectural quality. Johnson stands for the contemporary paradigm of the power of branding. While never having had anything original to 'say' in his architecture, his camp control of the spoken word controls architects in the capital of Capital, opinion and ambition. It is interesting that within his *côterie* there are neither academics nor critics, and once he discovered Eisenman's ability to reduce any complex thought to a few bullet points Johnson never had to read another book. Certainly this has not been through dyslexia.

New York comes across as being so unlike anywhere else that the Johnson phenomenon might appear unique. Elsewhere, however, architects form into tribes

Fame cuts across the categories of architectural quality. Johnson stands for the contemporary paradigm of the power of branding. While never having had anything original to 'say' in his architecture, his camp control of the spoken word controls architects in the capital of Capital, opinion and ambition.

cover of *Time*. Wright recognised Johnson's star quality in his celebrated put-down: 'Little Phil, do they allow you to put your buildings out in the weather?' Johnson's skills are entirely verbal unlike those of the other two, and in his dapper way he more resembles the public persona of the charismatic Wright. Like few other architects of such limited talent, he has succeeded in becoming a household name not just in America. Currently he is said to have had a hand in a projected shopping mall in Liverpool while publicly confessing that he has not visited the city since transatlantic liners left the city for the Americas.[3] He is promoted as a world-renowned architect, the penumbra of fame having been crafted by his own hand. When likened to Sir to control media and power. In London the dominance of Lord Rogers and his large extended family over the scenes of political patronage and policy resembles an oligarchy that extends from the mayoralty of London and the London School of Economics on the east side, through Whitehall via the impressive public relations operation of Arups, over to Hammersmith. Moreover, British urban regeneration activities now seem to be sadly dominated by the desire to enjoy flagship projects by signature architects, in order to provide regeneration for beacon councils through which urban improvements will trickle down to the deserving voters. Each adjective here – flagship, signature, beacon – indicates a sinister state of affairs that is evolving into a terrifying repetition of the disastrous housing policies of the 1950s and 1960s. Through 'fame', politicos and bureaucrats now have a list of mostly ennobled architects whose very presence on a letterhead is read as a guarantee of buying, as cheaply as possible, into the B effect. (B for Barcelona or Bilbao.) If flagship projects do not trickle down these same ennobled chaps can be blamed for the error. New York, London, Paris, Berlin, Tokyo, etc differ little in that the exercise of patronage appears to be controlled though the court may lack its king.

Fame is also necessarily fleeting. Unlike music, architecture cannot be replayed in a century's time because what is left are buildings, not musical scores. Bach will be ever fresh as long as interpreters and audiences find something in his music that speaks to them. Dead architects only get revivals. Many have been famous for a while, to be passed over later. Oh, I didn't know he was alive, comments the journo. Talent and quality need packaging to remain fresh. Packaging alone can prolong the sell-by date, as in the case of Johnson, but the fleeting character of fame has passed over stars of the 1960s whom it would be invidious to mention. Just as only very few pop groups – the Beatles or the Stones, for instance – can persist into their 60s, so architects are of limited interest to the public. Whether through luck or judgement, Rogers and Foster enjoy career trajectories such that, in their *troisième ages* when they could travel on public transport for a discount, they have taken on increasingly far-flung projects and engaged with larger scale urban commissions. The model for the young is, therefore, avoid too much too soon if you want to be famous and a grandparent.

The institution Architecture, once established to produce and reproduce itself, cannot avoid marketing within an increasingly transparent democracy. In parts of the profession the brass-plate argument still reigns. This posits that, once fully qualified, an architect should be able to put in public view a brass plate calling herself an architect. The public can then see that so-and-so offers a professional but not guaranteed level of service. And she sits by the phone waiting for the first call? Charming though this fantasy may be, and it still underpins the principles of architectural registration, the young architect needs publicity like a fish needs water. Publish, exhibit, network: these are the verbs leading to build. Previous ages depended upon more personal forms of patronage through accidents of birth, class and then genius. Today's Versailles architect phones, publishes and awards prizes. Wrapped in the glory of four-colour printing and monotone gossip, architectural reputations grow

and diminish in direct ratio to simple buzz questions like who's hot and who's not. If, therefore, the institution Architecture fails to recognise the transient but public world of marketing despite the discomfort of being packaged, then the sadomasochism of professionalism will be for real, not just for sex.

Finally, a few words on originality. The media matters more than the historian. What is now seen as original almost certainly has precedents that the media will not want to know about. That the work of what were once styled as Deconstructivist architects repeats the gestures of failed projects from Leninist Russia is a secret enjoyed by historians but ignored in the media. Originality in a pluralist, diverse world ceases to be a matter of reference and record, and depends instead on the shallow memory of the picture editor. If Gehry looks like Kiesler, Libeskind like early Gropius, Koolhaas like Leonidov, and even if they acknowledge their roots, the searchlight demanding originality operates outside of history. Vincent Scully wrote a book called *The Shingle Style Today; Or the Historian's Revenge*. All such works do is open up the copybook to those architects who had not already thought to look into it. Architects often refer to this as research, when actually they mean copying.

> Branding, marketing and being famous require only the appearance of originality. Its virtuality does not need heavy, ground-breaking creativity, though architectural mavens may temporarily discover this approach.

Coincidentally, architectural history is less fashionable amongst students now than it was 10 or 20 years ago.

Branding, marketing and being famous require only the appearance of originality. Its virtuality does not need heavy, ground-breaking creativity, though architectural mavens may temporarily discover this approach. But it does require robust abilities to brand and rebrand in order to keep that spotlight where it belongs. Such a requirement goes against the grain of artistic, and possibly architectural, practice insofar as the continuity of the individual producer's work rarely leaps from pinnacle to pinnacle in the course of a career. Rather, continuity is more like a career from career to career (Sondheim's *Follies*?). Perhaps architectural schools, one of the driving forces behind the institution Architecture – need courses in sustainable branding or how to court the court? ∆

David Dunster is Roscoe Professor of Architecture at the School of Architecture and Building Engineering, University of Liverpool.

Notes
1. James Collins, 'One Year Later: fashion finds a new star' (on Miguel Adrover), *The New Yorker* 16 April 2001), p 43.
2. These drawings were found by the author in the diaries of Edward Bennett and now reside in Bennett's archive in the Burnham Library of the Art Institute of Chicago.
3. The frontline architects are Studio BAAD and the site is on Chavasse Park, between the centre of Liverpool and the docks.
4. Philip Nobel, 'Johnson & Sons: The New Yorkers, *Architecture*, No 500 (December 2000), pp 122-3.
5. Vincent Scully, *The Shingle Style Today; Or; the Historian's Revenge*, George Brasiller (New York), 1974.

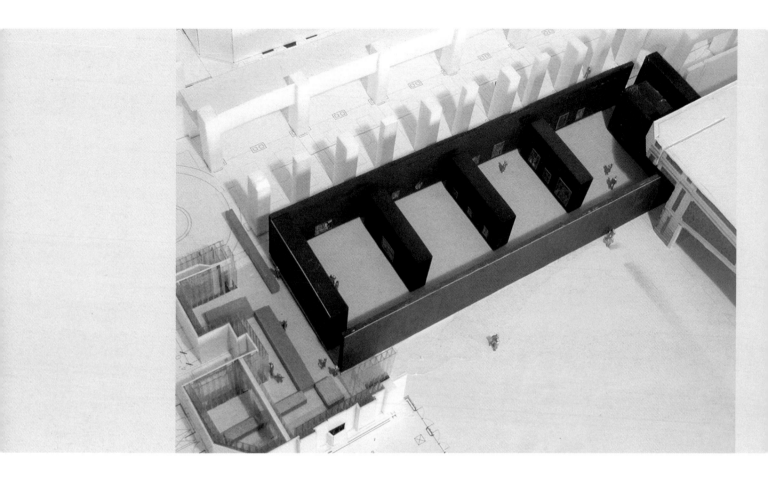

# Fame

versus

# Celebrity

As a critic and architectural historian, Charles Jencks concerns himself with lasting fame by identifying architects whose work is going to be of sufficient quality to outlive the most recent trends and fads and survive for posterity. In an interview with guest-editor Julia Chance, Jencks makes the distinction between fame and celebrity and expounds on just how contradictory, ambiguous and double-edged fame can be.

Opposite
OMA, view of the model for the Guggenheim Exhibition Hall in the Guggenheim Hermitage Museum, Las Vegas, completion 2001. Following on from its success with Frank Gehry's Bilbao, the Guggenheim is pursuing a strategy of globalisation - rendering each museum a star turn. Rem Koolhaas is an obvious choice for the gallery in terms of his star status, but also in terms of the building's unique situation. A freestanding building located within the Venetian Resort (a casino-hotel complex that pastiches historical Venice), it engenders an exciting interaction between high and popular culture.

Above
OMA, section of the main room in the Guggenheim Hermitage Musuem. Hangar-like, the main gallery has a 70-foot ceiling, a massive skylight, a functioning industrial crane, and additional lower level galleries. The floor of the ground level is flexible and may be opened to reveal a trench that drops down to lower-level galleries and spans the length of the exhibition space. The intention is to create a gallery with an elasticity of space that can accommodate any kind of exhibit or event.

Julia Chance: 'Fame' implies sometimes a deserved recognition for great accomplishments and at other times a more fleeting celebrity. Given that buildings are relatively complex and enduring products compared to say, pop songs, would you say that fame tends to be bestowed upon buildings and architects in the sense of a deserved and lasting recognition, or is it rather that the mass media reduces architecture to a series of photogenic images and sensational sound bytes ignoring its complexity?

Charles Jencks: Both aspects are mixed up in people's minds but they are in fact separate states. What I mean by that contradiction is apparent with Frank Gehry. He is the most famous architect in the world for fifteen minutes because of the New Guggenheim, and it appears in advertisements for going to Spain; it is the ultimate sound byte. And yet people go to Bilbao and spend the whole day involved with the building. Both conditions, fame and celebrity, occur at once. And that is what makes life exciting because the notion of what is called the 'knowing consumer', or the popular taste embracing Bilbao, shows that no matter how cynical you get, quality and invention are appreciated, and there is still a big audience for both.

JC: As a historian, would you comment on the relationship between architecture and fame in less media-dominated times?

CJ: Fame comes of course mostly in the west from the Romans, and the Latin derivation is *fari* which means 'to report that which people say or tell'. So it is based on the spoken word; to be talked about is to be famous. Its second meaning is a 'character attributed to a person', the notion that good reputation should be derived from great achievements. In these Roman definitions there is the positive notion of fame following the carrying out of great accomplishments and having them made permanent or immortal by architects, poets, writers and the every day talk of people. In other words, fame was considered at the very beginning to be divided between notoriety and something worthwhile. I think it is interesting that the fame game has always had this ambivalence.

The emperors always wanted to be immortal – as fascists do – and had Fora built to celebrate that idea of longevity. The empire consisted of a million people in Rome, which is a megalopolis, and so architecturally reinforced fame was an important way to get your power known about and asserted. There were strange emperors, like Caligula, who wanted to extend their fame through winning poetry and sports competitions. This was because in Roman parlance 'life is short and art is long'. It is interesting that you find an emperor having to cheat in those competitions to win more fame, which brings up the interesting relation between fame and infamy. I think the counterpart of fame, particularly today, is notoriety, or being famous for being famous, or famous for being stupid and drunk on TV like Tracey Emin. In other words, it starts off in Rome as ambivalent, and today the ambivalence has just deepened.

In all the arts there is the desire for lastingness and for immortality, and also the constant perversion of it. I can give you an example of something that is half way between the perversion and the reality by quoting Gio Ponti's article in June 1961, in *Domus* magazine, of which he was the editor. He worked for the fascists but he also did the Pirelli building which was the most famous modern building in Italy, and perhaps still is. Gio Ponti said,

'I grant and am pleased that architecture, good architecture, should be a means of advertising and I recommend it to all. When I happen to meet people who are ambitious to live on in history I never fail to advise them to invest in the bank of architecture which will assure them of a security which is their name of unfailing quotation, and I quote the benefits obtained by popes, kings, princes and patricians who loved architecture and whose names have remained in the splendour of history, and I quote what Mies and SOM have meant for Seagram and Lever House respectively.'

In a sense Ponti is heir to the Roman emperors and the whole idea that architects build to make their client famous. Also, remember that the Medici commissioned Brunelleschi and Alberti to build them their palace in the centre of Florence and they said, 'we cannot build this palace because it will make everybody too envious, and envy is a flower one should never water'. It is interesting that the Medici turned down an important building for precisely the reasons of envy. Of course Florence in the Renaissance was a hot bed of jealousy.

This shows that architecture has always been a funny mode of display, of 'Do I, or do I not?', 'Does the client or doesn't the client want fame?'. Movie stars suffer this problem the most. If you tour movie stars homes in Los Angeles, (there are Movie Star maps for this purpose sold on the street corner), then you can see they are caught between the desperate desire to advertise themselves and an even greater desire to be private. The result of this contradiction is that they get the worst architects

to do them pompous buildings, which are *also* unobtrusive. They say 'look at me but do not look at me because I'm worthless'. It is the strangest inversion of the sign.

JC: Pierre Bourdieu proposes that the logic of the cultural field operates to increase, legitimate and to reproduce the class structure which he views as being a system of inequality. This is relevant when considering architecture and the phenomenon of fame because it suggests that there may be patterns or tendencies underlying the way in which certain architects or kinds of architecture are propelled to fame. Is architecture assessed in the restrictive terms of the legitimate culture or do you think there is such a thing as independently great architecture that cuts through, in Bourdieuvian terms, the objectively existing social structures?

CJ: I think that Hannes Meyer and the Marxists are right in the sense that, as Meyer said, 'Never forget architecture is built for the ruling class'. That is true, but it doesn't mean that therefore it is always corrupting or corrupt, or necessarily anti-the public, or the working class, or other groups. That is an old left wing response. The constraints of class and power are real, but within those limits buildings can be resistant to the dominant. They can engender moods, feelings and ideas which are subversive to the dominant and to degraded power. They cannot change the class structure, and when architecture is seen to be a tool to change power relations it is almost invariably negative. Architects must take a position about power and class but they cannot believe ideologically that they are the spearhead of cultural and economic revolution because, if they do, they are likely to end up with false consciousness and torture themselves and their clients into buildings that people hate. The failure of modernism is the public housing foisted on the people in the name of the people – 'Let us give the people what we think they need'. It was not always what they needed or *wanted* and that is one of the problems of ideological architecture.

Yes architecture probably does insidiously support the class structure but it can also insidiously critique the class structure, so therefore all culture is not always supportive of the class structure. You could say *anything* that you pay for is supporting the exploitation of workers, the exchange value – yes. But a barter society also has power structures. Anyway, I think that Bourdieu may have overstated the way culture legitimises power. Perhaps it is more true of the French situation where you have the state, the classical class structures and Marxism all marching together in lock-step, and so the structure works as in Bourdieu's theory; they all perform according to Marxist theory. But the world is not like the French performers. Adriaan Geuze's work with West 8 in Amsterdam is a

*Die von der Zeit getragene Fama.*
*Es muß zwar meinen Schall, der Ruhm, und Lob erwirbt,*
*So lang noch Menschen sind, die graue Zeit erhalten:*
*Doch halt ich wiederum, was ihre Hand Verdirbt;*
*Ich, die ich übrig bin, Wenn alles muß veralten.*

*La renommée Soutenüe par le temps.*
*Mon cri, qui d'un chacun rend la gloire publique,*
*est à la verité Soutenu par le tems*
*Mais tout ceque detruit Son regne tyrannique*
*trouve chez moi un nom immortel et constant.*

liberating, pluralist although market-orientated mixture of workers' housing, middle class housing, and a few rich houses. What can Bourdieu say about that?

As Post-Marxists, Baudrillard and Bourdieu have opened a new discussion. They say that culture shows the system recapitulates itself, but today it is done through symbolic signs rather than economics. These are important insights into the mediated society, but perhaps they overstate the case; because culture always has the freedom from this direct feedback that they imply. The cultural sign, because it is ambiguous, multi-layered and out of control is not just a reification of the class system or money. Sometimes culture runs away and gets out of control. You cannot say that Gehry's New Guggenheim in Bilbao just supports the system. The 'Bilbao effect' is a good example of the way famous architects can open up so many clients around the world – and architects – to new kinds of thinking. It was a wild card that Frank played. Of course, it was a capitalist card because it was the most prestigious commission in the late 20th century. The Guggenheim museum, furthermore, is an off-shore, lend-lease, multi-national museum, and a grab for power by Tom Krens the chairman, and he was wise to choose Gehry. It serves the interests of capitalism, so Bourdieu is right there; but it is also opening other doors

and liberating. So more than one thing happens and that is characteristic of cultural things. Their logic is not, as Jameson and Baudrillard want to say, reductive.

JC: A significant number of ex-architectural students complain of having been fed a myth during their years of study - that they were the superstars of the future. On emerging into the workplace they found that the apparent routes to stardom had vanished and that in no time they became fodder for the building industry or the very ordinary designer of buildings. There is much to say for this position on both sides, but the point is that they were delivered a false idea about their future while studying. How do you think that architecture schools deal with the phenomenon of fame?

CJ: Badly. I agree with them: there is a great deal of unrealism around about all of this. First of all historically, only about one per cent of the environment has ever been designed by architects. So architects have never had much power, and maybe they shouldn't. Maybe you should be taught in architecture schools not to be expressive, but taught that you are actually in a craft, in a service and not in an art form, and therefore what is expected of you in 99 per cent of your buildings is just carrying out the wishes of your client.

On the other hand, who would go into such a field? It sounds like plumbing! You cannot say glorified plumbing is what the role of architecture has been historically. The role has always been to crystallise the values and ideals of a culture and to present them back, to mirror those values. And that of course is a starring

role. Imhotep, the first architect in 2800BC for Pharaoh Djoser, is already into the fame game and asked to design that superstar stepped pyramid. That is what architecture is about. Art students have a similar problem of asymmetry: there is only one Damien Hirst, and should they be taught that painting is really painting walls? Or should they all aspire to be Damien Hirst?

If I were the head of a school and could have a revolution in the schools, I would teach economics and social realism and how society really works. Then I would teach, as some firms do like KPF, how to get the job and keep it. KPF actually convinced clients to leave Philip Johnson for them. They found out that Philip Johnson had a $20m building and they said, 'you think you've got the best? We can do better than Philip'. They took the job right away from him. Now that is competitive, capitalist training and it ought to be part of the way ethics is taught in schools – when is it stealing jobs, when is it legitimate, when should you wait until an architect is fired etc. All these are ethical and difficult issues that are not addressed. It would be hard to do so, because the students would rebel, the Marxists would rebel and theoretically people would have great trouble with calling a spade a spade. But I think that we do hurt students by not being realistic about what really is happening in society.

I would also teach the history of lasting fame. That in effect is what I write about as a critic and as a historian, to identify the people who are going to be lasting and have quality. What else is architecture for after all? Building can satisfy all our other requirements, but architecture should last. And this is different from branding, with which it is often confused.

JC: What advice would you give to contemporary architects in terms of negotiating the phenomena of fame?

CJ: HH Richardson said in the 19th century, "the first principle of architecture is to get the job and the second principle is to keep it". The difficulty for an architect today is that fame is one of the most important ways in which you get the job, and once you are famous you get jobs simply because you are famous. So it is a circular, self-confirming hypothesis. Architects are famous because they're famous.

Furthermore, architects have to reinvent themselves every ten years. After the cognitive scientist Howard Gardner, I call it the 'ten year rule'; this transformation is necessary because technology, society and fashion change, real things change, and to stay on top you have to reinvent yourself, as Le Corbusier shows, every 10 years.

However, the architect is in this curious contradictory position, like the movie star, like Greta Garbo, because to get the job they have to be somewhat famous and hard to get at the same time. But they cannot advertise, and advertisement would be considered an admission of

Above
Supermarket selling Michael Graves's merchandise.

Opposite
Philip Johnson and the First Eight, 1980, as featured in the book *Kings of Infinite Space* by Charles Jencks (Academy Editions, 1983).

method. Or, like Peter Eisenman, you can run a series of international seminars in which you have 10 critics writing you up every six months. Peter told me five years ago in New York, 'Look you are dead if you do not have an agent. And you are dead if your agent isn't keyed into *The New York Times* and the five critics who count'.

Branding is a reality, and the young are so conscious of its downside. Without fame you do not get fortune, and so if you want to be a success then you have to be famous you have to become a brand – a vicious circle. There is no easy answer, but it is important to bring all of these motivations into consciousness, because it is producing a branding type of architect like Philippe Starck – who's actually rather good at both branding and giving a good product.

Duchamp said, 'the fame of an artist depends on the multiplication of small anecdotes'. If everything is mediated today then fame no longer means to be talked about so much as to be written about, and reproduced in a photograph and in a by-line. It almost doesn't matter what is said. That is why Oscar Wilde's quote is so poignant today, because if you aren't talked about, you are dead! He was referring to high society, but today that has become a horrible truth for professionals. On the other hand, you could say that is not true because if you get a solid enough practice then your reputation does not depend on entering the celebrity game. You can sustain clients without having to do strange, torturous things. But the media is always there. Frank Lloyd Wright showed that in 1938 when he finished the Johnson Wax Building. Wright said to his client, 'Look I've given you two million dollars worth of advertising by being on the cover of *Time* and ten other magazines. It is worth two million and I should charge you for it!'.

Today, writers have to have an agent, they have to keep their name in the public, these are realities. But this is not done for fame, so much as selling, and if they think it is for fame it will be the fifteen minute variety. Nothing is more old hat than yesterday's celebrity. Fame and its problematic have always been around and the people who ultimately lasted had quality and they got it by long slow research and fighting. Daniel Libeskind was 20 years in the wilderness, Rem was 20 and Gehry was 30 years. They got to be famous through creativity, hard work and suffering.

Fame is clearly double-edged. FR Leavis, George Steiner and many critics believe 'you either want to live forever, or you are going to be an inferior writer'. They have a point. ♾

defeat, would only make you notorious. Yet in a mass media society people forget you almost immediately if you are not on the scene. It is unfortunate, but if you disappear from the scene for six months people think that you are dead, so you have to keep your name in front of the public in some way and make appearances. At the same time you cannot be seen to advertise, or to be overt about it, so you have to pretend that you aren't really doing it. I think that is why when I talked to Frank Gehry about being interviewed for this publication he said 'no, no I do not want to, I do not want to know about it'. It is a taboo, something that architects do not want to confront. And yet as Oscar Wilde said, 'there is only one thing in the world that is worse than being talked about, and that is not being talked about'.

Architects are knowing victims in this situation. Greta Garbo became famous, like Charles Saatchi, by hiding herself and that works only if you are *seen and known* to be hiding yourself. Architects think or want to think that they're above the game, as anyone does, and yet they live in a society which because of the media is infinitely forgetful. Therefore the ways out of that conundrum are either to overproduce a lot of buildings and then to get them written about, or to write a lot of books. The big books of Rem Koolhaas are a good example of the second

# The Architect,
# Conspicuousness
## and the Part Played by
# Fame

The definition of what constitutes an 'architect' and ideas about 'fame' have changed radically over time, shifting with each particular cultural context. While at times eminence has been regarded as the essential quality of fame, at others it has been prominence. Here, Royston Landau provides a brief historical overview, which highlights key points in the history of the western architect, while also making particular reference to styles of conspicuousness.

The ninth millennium BC saw the beginning of built human settlements and by the third millennium grandiose structures were being produced, such as the Egyptian step pyramid at Sakkara for the pharaoh Djoser (2800 BC). This was reputedly designed by the 'architect' (also physician) Imhotep, who would later be made a demigod. Although there is little evidence of Imhotep's identity, or of the role he played in the design of the pyramid, we can assume that he was a person of high eminence in Egypt's social hierarchy. At this stage in history, a structure such as the step pyramid indicates that new geometries, new technologies and new constructional skills were being developed, presumably by a sophisticated community that was capable of producing a religious/political symbol that could exalt the life of Djoser as a king and as a god. This first pyramid marked the earliest stages of the great Egyptian architecture to come, whose buildings included pyramids and temples.

A new temple tradition was developed in ancient Greece, but it was the fifth century BC – more than 2,000 years after Sakkara – before the Greek temple reached its peak of perfection on the Acropolis at Athens. Commissioned by Pericles (490–429 BC), the Acropolis buildings included the Erectheion, the Propylaea gateway and the Parthenon. A temple of Athena was removed to make way for the Erectheion.

The Parthenon – the temple of Athena Parthenos – was built under the orders of Pericles and its construction was supervised by Phidias, the sculptor who was also in charge of its statues and figures. These remain among the greatest achievements of Greek art. Ictinus and Callicrates, the Parthenon's architects, used the Doric order to achieve a level of refinement that would never again be equalled. This greatly talented design community formed a part of the Athenian elite which produced some of the highest intellectual achievements Europe has ever known. Although the buildings that remain tell us much about ancient Greek architecture, there is little evidence to indicate just how

architects thought about their architecture. However, written evidence has survived from the Roman period, so we know more.

An architectural text that would greatly influence future European architecture was written between 50 and 30 BC by the Roman engineer/architect Vitruvius (90–20 BC). Dedicated to the emperor Augustus, it attempted to describe the whole domain of architecture as Vitruvius knew it. His qualifications for such a task were unusual. After some modest house-building experience followed by work in ballistic engineering, he joined the Roman army as an engineering adviser and invented and built important catapult equipment. He hence became known to Julius Caesar and took part in his military campaigns between 58 and 44 BC. He travelled widely and had personal contact with Caesar himself. After Caesar's assassination in 44 BC Vitruvius retired from the army and with the help of Caesar's heir, Augustus, and on the recommendation of Augustus' elder sister Octavia, he received a pension in order to prepare a comprehensive text on architecture. This was his *De architectura*. In its 10 volumes he expressed high expectations for architectural education and learning when he wrote that the architect must be, 'skilful with the pencil, instructed in geometry, know much history, have followed the philosophers with attention, understand music, have knowledge of medicine, know the opinions of the jurist, be acquainted with astronomy and the theory of the heavens'.[1] He then described, in more than 160 chapters, what he believed the well-informed designer should know.

In spite of his comprehensive text, Vitruvius achieved no fame and little recognition in Rome and it appears that he never connected with the main body of Roman architects.[2] However, a millennium and a half later, his text would not only survive but it would become a paradigm for the Italian Renaissance culture.

In the Gothic period the autonomous architect with the widely aspiring Vitruvian education did not exist. Societies were dominated by religion and found intellectual independence unacceptable. Within this context mainly anonymous and uncelebrated, but highly skilled, craftsman/builders emerged to construct cathedrals and church-related buildings. In the later Gothic period they were required to join guilds which imposed strict regulative rules.

Opposite
The first Egyptian pyramid, the step pyramid at Sakkara, was constructed for the pharaoh Djoser (2800 BC). It was reputedly built by the 'architect' and physician Imhotep, whose fame and eminence were such that he was eventually promoted to the status of demigod.

Above
The designers of the
Parthenon in Athens
(447–433 BC) came from
the Athenian intellectual
elite. The architects of the
fine Doric temple were Ictinus
and Callicrates and the entire
project was supervised by
the sculptor Phidias, who was
responsible for the temple's
sculptures including the
renowned Elgin marbles.

Opposite
Brunelleschi's design for the
dome of Florence Cathedral
(c. 1419–36) epitomised the
pragmatic individualism of
Renaissance Italy. A great
engineering feat, the cupola
spans 138 feet without the aid
of centering. This vast space
over the duomo's crossing
had been ambitiously provided
by the cathedral's builders
at the end of the 13th century
when there was no known
means of covering it.

Renaissance Italy of the early 15th century
saw the architect/artist increasingly
individualised in a culture that encouraged
exploration. In 1434 Filippo Brunelleschi
(1377–1446) was constructing what was then the
largest ever dome, for the Santa Maria del Fiore
cathedral in Florence. Already a famous
architect, he strongly disapproved of the
autocratic builders' guild, to which he was
required to belong and contribute. In protest, he
refused to pay his dues. The guild prosecuted
him and had him sent to prison. The Church
leaders immediately challenged this and
Brunelleschi was released without further
liability after only 11 days. This represented a
victory for the artist to be a, 'free man to look
after himself and act as his conscience
dictated'.[3] It was evidence that the 400-year-old
Gothic domination was ending and was being
supplanted by a new Renaissance culture that
relished individual artistic talent and assigned fame
where it was thought to be due.

The Vitruvian writings were used as a model by
Leone Battista Alberti (1404–72). Alberti was a scholar,
a humanist and a widely knowledgeable architect and
his *De re aedificatoria* (1485) was a highly coordinated
and didactic, rather than descriptive, treatise. It was
written in elegant Latin (to be distinguished from
Vitruvius's ad hoc texts which, according to Alberti,
were written in bad Latin). During Alberti's lifetime the
text was available only in handwritten form, so it could
only be read by the educated and rich elite to whom it
was addressed. But shortly after his death a new media
dimension – the 'printed book' – arrived. This changed
the idea of an architectural text. Drawings could now be
reproduced; and books were more widely read.

A major text which depended upon illustrations and
would not have been possible before printing was *Tutte
l'opere d'architettura* by Sebastiano Serlio (1475–1554).
Serlio worked in Rome from c1514 and in 1527, after

**Notes**
1. Morris Hickey Morgan, *Vitruvius: the Ten Books of Architecture*, Dover (New York), 1960, p 5.
2. A century after Vitruvius's death, Sextus Julius Frontinus (AD c40–103) dedicated his book on Roman waterworks, *De Acquis Urbis Romae*, to him – Vitruvius was remembered not as an architect, but as someone who had contributed to water engineering.
3. Rudolf and Margaret Wittkower, *Born under Saturn*, WW Norton (London and New York),1969, p 10.
4. The role of the developer builder in 18th-century London is discussed in John Summerson, *Georgian London*, Pleiades Books (London), 1945; Pelican Books (London), 1962.

the sack of the city by Charles V, he moved to Venice, Italy's leading book-printing centre. Unlike Alberti's treatise, Serlio's illustrated texts, in eight books, were practical instruction manuals for designers and builders, written in *volgare* (spoken Italian) which was understandable by a wide working audience. Later published in Dutch, English and German, Serlio's text was a major source of reference in 16th- and 17th-century Italy and was much used until the mid-19th century. Other Renaissance treatises had different agendas. Vignola (1507–73) concentrated on his interpretation of the greatest examples of the classical orders, while Palladio (1508–80) illustrated his own architecture as well as the many Roman buildings that had inspired him. Printed texts became a prime source of information and the means to achieve conspicuousness and gain fame.

Printed texts became a prime source of information and the means to achieve conspicuousness and gain fame.

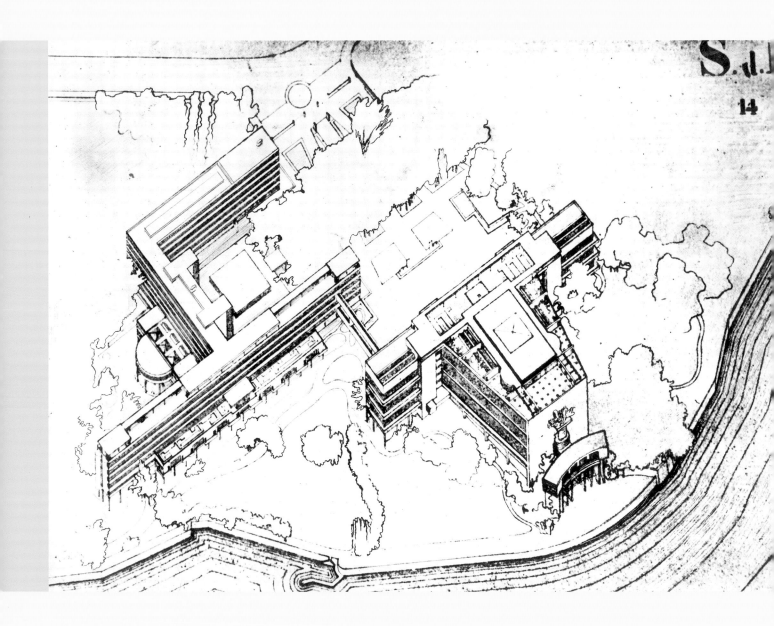

The CIAM story provides evidence of the emergence of the new 'free designer', a person who is no longer committed to any common style or agenda but who, by wishing to survive, needs to achieve conspicuousness in an increasingly globalised world.

5. Robert Adam's first book, *The Ruins of the Palace of the Emperor Diocletian at Spalatro* (1764), was prepared while he was on a Grand Tour of Italy (1755–57). It was planned to be a means to gain conspicuousness when he returned to take up residence in London. The book was an elegantly produced publication, printed in Venice, bound in Rome, illustrated by Clérisseau and dedicated to George II and, when he died, George III. Robert Adam's second text, written with his brother James, was *The Works in Architecture of Robert and James Adam* (1773–78).

6. Le Corbusier's idea, the Athens Charter classified the problems of the modern city (in 1933) under four main headings – dwellings, recreation, work and transportation – to which was added a fifth one: historic buildings.

7. The changing and new interaction and close connection between the architect, the user and the user's products is described under the heading 'doorstep philosophy'. See Alison Smithson (ed), *Team 10 Primer*, the MIT Press (Cambridge MA), 1968, p 96.

8. The earliest Team 10 members included Bakema, Candilis, Gutmann, Alison and Peter Smithson, Howell, van Eyck and Voelcker. Later members included Shadrach Woods, De Carlo, Coderch, Pologni, Soltan and Wewerka.

9. In not attending CIAM 10 at Dubrovnik, Le Corbusier wrote a letter saying that 'the metamorphosis should be based upon the new generation' and defining who the new generation should be. Gropius apologised saying that he was too busy to attend (there is evidence that this was not true). Van Eesteren wrote a letter saying that, 'the new influence should go its own way and that the constitution of CIAM should regard its specific task as ended.' See Royston Landau, 'The end of CIAM and the Role of the British', The Last CIAMs, *Rassegna*, 52 (December1992), pp 40–7.

10. After CIAM 10, Team 10 member Jakob Bakema organised a different type of conference in 1960, at Otterlo in Holland which included Louis Kahn (1901–74), who had been much disapproved of by the CIAM bosses.

Opposite
Le Corbusier's drawing for the League of Nations Headquarters at Geneva, 1937. Its rejection, for political reasons, in the competition to design the building provided the catalyst for the forum which was to become CIAM.

The effect of Renaissance architecture on that in 18th-and 19th-century Britain was significant. Although Georgian London was dominated commercially by developer builders[4] there was also a small number of outstanding architects, each with a particular 'classical' agenda – and each of whom also participated in activities other than architecture. Robert Adam (1728–92), for example, was a Member of Parliament, a building contractor, an owner of 'patents', a property developer and an author[5] as well as an architect. However, the 19th century saw the beginnings of a decrease in the scope of the architect as the architectural body of knowledge increased and new specialisations emerged.

In 1828 civil engineers professionalised themselves, as did architects (the Institute of British Architects) in 1836. More new building disciplines followed including chartered surveyors, mechanical engineers, structural engineers, electrical engineers (founded 1886), quantity surveyors, town planners, urban designers and landscape architects, each of whom set up its own professional institute. The divisions between these disciplines were further strengthened by academic programmes, created by external institutions, for each new specialisation. The result was that when the professions approved and 'validated' their educational programmes, they also constrained and controlled the scope and the content of that education.

With increasing internationalisation and advances in communicating through the media, the potential for conspicuousness grew in the 20th century. Le Corbusier (1887–1965), always conscious of the importance of being seen and heard, widely publicised such projects as his Ville Contemporaine for three million inhabitants (1922), many modern-style houses, manifestos and articles, but it was his failure to win the League of Nations Headquarters Competition in 1927, allegedly because the project was modernist, that caused him to promote a forum that would become the Congrès Internationaux d'Architecture Moderne (CIAM).

The first ever-successful multinational architectural organisation, in the 1930s CIAM had a relatively small international attendance. After the Second World War, however, it was more widely attended although Le Corbusier's Athens Charter,[6] which had dominated CIAM debates since CIAM 4 in 1933, started to be contested. Increasingly strong criticism grew from a 'younger' generation of architects who had experienced the war and saw CIAM as possessing an authoritarian approach and the Athens Charter as laying down rules that were oversimplistic and less than relevant. Instead, a new focus was proposed that would not tell people what was good for them but would be about consultation and learning through a process of architect/user interaction.[7] A small group of highly active 'younger' members, later to be called Team 10[8] and brought together to prepare for the 10th Congress, held in Dubrovnik (then in Yugoslavia), highlighted the intellectual problems CIAM was facing, through publications as well as through their own conspicuousness. It had already been acknowledged before this congress that the differences between the elders and the youngers had reached an irresolvable stage, and Le Corbusier, Walter Gropius and van Eesteren chose not attend it.[9] Nevertheless, CIAM 10 was a discordant meeting and although there was one further non-CIAM attempt, in 1960, to assemble the architectural community at Otterlo in Holland[10] this stage in the history of architecture had ended.

The CIAM story provides evidence of the emergence of the new 'free designer', a person who is no longer committed to any common style or agenda but who, by wishing to survive, needs to achieve conspicuousness in an increasingly globalised world.

But this must be another story. ⚙

Royston Landau AA.Dipl, RIBA, is Emeritus Director of the Architectural Association Graduate School. Publications include: 'Towards a structure for architectural ideas', *Arena*, vol 81, no 893 (June 1965); *New Directions in British Architecture*, Braziller, (New York), 1968; guest-editor, 'Thinking about Architecture', *Architectural Design*, (September 1969); 'Notes on the concept of an architectural position', *AA Files*, no1, (1981); 'Enquiring into the architectural agenda', *Journal of Architectural Education*, vol 40, no 2 (1987); 'The history of modern architecture that still needs to be written', *AA Files*, no 21 (1991); 'Architecture, Ethics and the Person' in Martha Pollak (ed], *The Education of the Architect*, The MIT Press (Cambridge MA), 1997; 'Architectural History and the Present Condition' in At Fortaelle Arkitektur, Arkitektens Forlag (Copenhagen), 2000.

# Functional Icons

## Charles Jencks in Conversation with Lord Foster

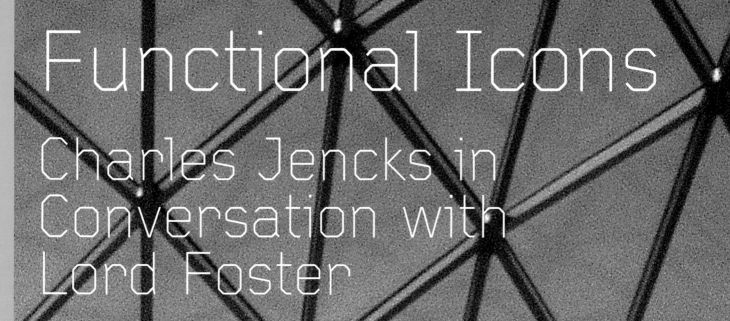

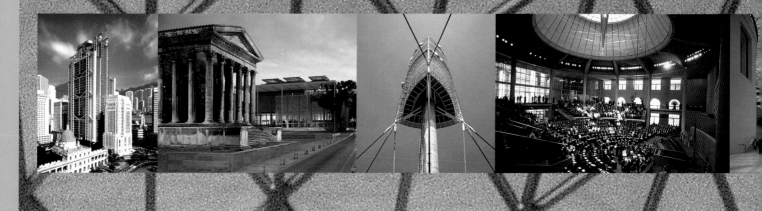

Lord Foster of Thames Bank is probably the most famous architect in Britain. The recipient of the Royal Gold Medal for Architecture in 1983, he became the 21st Pritzker Architecture Prize Laureate in 1999. Granted a knighthood in the 1990 Queen's Birthday Honours List,

he was appointed the Order of Merit in 1997 and in 1999 was honoured with a Life Peerage. Here, Charles Jencks discusses with Lord Foster his major contribution to architecture, his main iconic works, and his own take on fame, celebrity and publicity.

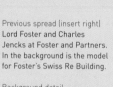

CJ: Norman, I want to ask you about the question of fame, one that is exercising *Architectural Design* and others at the moment. Vitruvius in the first century BC writes about the importance of fame in getting the job and keeping it. He has a wonderfully ridiculous description of how Dinocrates got to be the architect for Alexander the Great. The frustrated designer happened to have a good physique and 'pleasing countenance' so naturally he took advantage of these qualities. He subtracted his clothes, anointed his body with oil, threw a lion's skin over his left shoulder and went up to the king, who at the time, was in front of the tribunal, administering justice. Naturally Dinocrates stood out from the crowd, was invited to explain himself to the king, and offered up the most flattering design: a whole city that looked like Alexander the Great. The rest is history, as they say, or at least Alexandria.

It's a ridiculous story, but within the history of

architecture there is a developed relationship to fame, because architecture is supposed to make permanent, or celebrate, that which is important. One should distinguish between celebrity and fame. Since Andy Warhol famously said that, in the future everybody will be world-famous for fifteen minutes, fame has turned into column inches. That's one of our problems – your problem, my problem, everybody's problem. Because *People Magazine* and personality journalism have co-opted the concept of fame, it has been reduced to commerce and notoriety. However, fame for the Romans had to do with immortality, and outlasting the ephemera of the moment. Basically the notion that life is short, art is long. Art confers longevity, creates immortality and long term memory, and that is why the Renaissance built its big buildings. So fame has these positive and negative associations – I think you would probably agree with all that.

### The iconic and the ephemeral
If we jump to the present and look at your buildings, you can find similar motivation, especially with the iconic buildings since the Hongkong and Shanghai Bank. Symbolic depth and striking iconic form create buildings that last, which are famous in a positive sense. Obviously, the Reichstag is a very iconic building – meant to be long lasting and symbolic – and the Great Court at the British Museum. Then there's the Glasgow convention centre; the two buildings in London, for Swiss Re and GLA; the Médiathèque in Nimes, the Barcelona Tower, possibly the Commerzbank in Frankfurt, and certainly the Music Centre at Gateshead. Maybe 10 of your buildings in the last ten years have been iconic buildings. What do you feel about this and symbolism in general?
NF: I think that we've also, in parallel, been producing the most ephemeral building. Take the Computer Technology office – an air-supported structure that in 1970 was erected in 55 minutes and which was removed in about the same time. Similarly, what also promised to be an ephemeral head office for IBM, which took all the parameters of temporary accommodation and

**Above**
Interior view of the Great Court at the British Museum, London, 1994–2000. This new covered courtyard reclaims the court at the centre of the museum that was lost in the middle of the 19th century with the insertion of the new Reading Room of the British Library. By enclosing the space surrounding the central reading room with a lightweight glazed roof, Foster and Partners have not only created a public heart to the museum – open from early in the morning to late at night – but also rationalised the museum's entry and circulation.

produced an instant building, has endured.

CJ: You mean IBM Cosham?

NF: Yes. It was described by Alan McDadd, the Head of Real Estate at IBM some five years afterwards as the only building that IBM would replace if its entire stock of buildings were to burn down. I suspect that was because it was the only one that was non-specific and flexible. Significantly at the time, it also gained a kind of iconic status.

CJ: It did indeed.

NF: In the same way, the industrial building for Renault, which also came out of what I would call the anonymous tradition, played a key role in the company's advertising.

CJ: You are committed equally to both long-lasting and ephemeral buildings?

NF: We always have been. I would suggest that the boundaries between permanent and ephemeral are today far less clear cut.

CJ: So symbolism is equally on the ephemeral and permanent sides. Fair enough: Andy Goldsworthy makes monuments out of stone, as well as icicles and things that last as long as the ice doesn't melt. So you also see that an ephemeral thing can also be culturally long-lasting, although temporally short-lived.

NF: Yes, exactly.

CJ: I ask you this partly because, as a Modern architect, I suppose you have a deep suspicion of two things. First is the monument – the monumental focus, the historical monument, especially in the 19th century sense. Second is a wariness for things that are self-consciously imposed from outside the building task, put on buildings for either historical or cultural reasons. In other words, you design from the inside-out, from the functional side of the building task. You have always made it your purpose to know the client's needs, perhaps even more completely than they do themselves. So you would hate to think of designing from the

preconception, or *à priori* first. With the Swiss Re, for instance, you did not set out to design a "gherkin", as it's mis-labelled, and you don't usually design with iconic shapes.

NF: I think that you search for as many anchors or as many generators as you can find... Anybody who is trying to optimise on a design opportunity is simultaneously thinking of the problems from many different vantage points, inside and out. If you take the British Museum and the Great Court, I'd have to think to identify the most powerful generator. Is it more important that it is a space open outside museum hours, a meeting place, an event on an important route through the city, or a museum within a museum, or an urban room existing outside the context of the British Museum as a museum. But you have to move from outside to inside and analyse the incredible internal problems of the museum. There was an entrance hall that was probably adequate for a few hundred people 150 years ago. By the 1990s it was inundated with six and a half million people a year, and the only way they could get into one gallery was to go through another gallery, so it was a nightmare. How do you regenerate that, how do you bring a new sense of order, clarity, convenience ... ?

CJ: But that's the classic Modern Movement answer.

NF: You say "classic Modern Movement answer" – I find that difficult because it smacks of easy categorisation – you may know what you mean, but I don't. I think that is your interpretation!

CJ: Your approach is 'design from the inside out.'

NF: No – from both inside outwards and outside inwards – some aspects of both can be statistically measured and some cannot – they are all value judgements.

CJ: No, no, it's real – you are a Modernist, and I think you probably think you are too – more or less – although you have moved on and have other concerns. And I don't mean that either negatively or positively, but I'm trying to get the discussion into another space. In the Modern Movement, of course, there was, among other positions, the question of understatement – the silent butler approach to architecture.

NF: I think I know what you might be trying to say. But, for example, it was absolutely conscious for us to assert that the Reichstag, in its rebirth, in the transformation of its function, should make its stamp on the skyline. From the outside, it had to symbolically announce on the skyline that the interior use of the building had changed. In other words, it was no longer the burnt-out symbol of a past imperialism. That image is now branded in the public consciousness – it is a universal backdrop – whether in television news, advertising or front-page journalism.

Similarly it is also significant that overnight the Commerzbank appeared on the front page of the

The New German Parliament, The Reichstag, Berlin, 1992–99. Foster and Partners' commission to reconstruct the Reichstag was the result of their winning an invited competition in 1993. The guiding principles of the scheme were public accessibility and procedural openness. These are epitomised by the glazed dome that symbolises transparency and provides a view of the city and the Bundestag when they are sitting below.

Above left
Exterior view showing the cupola and part of the roof.

Above right
Interior general view of the cupola.

*Financial Times* as the symbol of Frankfurt as a financial centre alongside the financial index. In the same way the external image of the Hongkong Bank became a symbol.

CJ: Right, and so it dominates the currency – the Hong Kong dollar, to give it support.

NF: It was a symbol of confidence in the future of that colony – of its stability ...

CJ: Right, but let's talk about the availability of buildings to become symbols. Why, let us say, the Commerzbank, the Hong Kong Shanghai Bank, the Reichstag and a few others became symbols for a city ...

NF: Barcelona ...

CJ: Barcelona, exactly. You obviously have in your armoury a theory and a practice of how symbols, which are integral, can emerge. The one word that you do use about Gaudì is integrity. This is another way in which I find, very strangely, that you and I share several deep commitments. One of my favourite architects is Gaudì, and I find to my surprise that you've written good things about him. We also share things about cosmic symbolism. Perhaps we also agree – if this is your position – that in order for symbols to emerge they must have a certain depth; in order to have that depth they have to be based on necessities, of the function of the building, of the reality, and mediate that with larger concerns. In other words, you must design from the inside-out in order for a symbol to have resonance. On the other hand – but I don't want to fetishise our differences! – it seems to me an architect also has a commitment to the public consumption of symbols which are historic and in which there is an independent factor that comes from the sensibility. Le Corbusier's interest in women, let us say, or the sun's path – these symbols come out of his paintings, his experience, alchemy. But those kinds of references you don't allow yourself.

NF: I'm not at all sure that's accurate.

CJ: Except in the overall shape.

NF: Well, it would be difficult to conceive of the roof of the Reichstag without its solar dimension. The shading eyebrow – that vast equivalent of a pair of sunglasses – rotates around the edge of the circular ramp, following the sun – even powered by its rays, which are converted through photovoltaic panels into electricity. Then there are the mirrors – they celebrate the sky and its solar dimension – beaming out at night the message of democracy at work.

CJ: ... up to the sky – the open-air oculus as the culmination of a route, like the Pantheon.

NF: That was the conscious intention. The use of cables at Barcelona can be seen to work in the same way – arguably not the first of its kind of those sorts of structures – but in that location almost visually silent. The tower is in effect ephemeralised almost to the point of absurdity; the idea that a whole building could be poised on an ultra-thin stalk marking the top of a mountain, invisibly supported on ever so discreet cables.

CJ: That is a Constructivist symbol, like the Skylon.

NF: It's a symbol, nevertheless. Who am I to say that there isn't a thread of symbolic recognition of their importance running through all the projects?

CJ: I grant that.

### Swiss Re and symbolism

CJ: Though its been called a gherkin, the Swiss Re is more obviously like a cigar or a missile in terms of its multiple layering. It uses the design concept of an egg. The egg has been used as a model to generate the building, in the way that orange peels generated the Sydney Opera House. That is the most iconic building in Sydney, the symbol of its renewal, and your Swiss Re will be iconic in London. So I ask you how you see its symbolism? Although the gherkin reading is fun, and shows it's a pop building like all new, strong shapes, how do you want it to be read, publicly?

NF: Well, in one sense it has this dismissive element, journalistically; but it's interesting that it captures the imagination to the extent that somebody thinks it's important enough for them to have to label it.

CJ: Like it or not, anything that is unusual and striking

will call forth new metaphors. If I were in your position and felt it was being misread, I would blast off a letter saying: 'No, you fools, don't you see it's a pinecone – or a pineapple!'

NF: Maybe it's better that somebody else does that. It carries more authority. The building comes out of considered responses to the perceived needs of the City of London and Swiss Re. This is seen in the way it is generated internally, and is seen from the outside and the ecological issue, the way in which it can create a more benign interior environment. We've seen the other buildings through which Swiss Re has evolved – the stepping stones that have gone before, the Bank, the Tokyo Millennium Tower, and the Commerzbank with its four-storey-high gardens that spiral, all nine of them, and change their vegetation depending on the direction they face, and the different types – the Asian garden, the North American garden, the Mediterranean garden …

CJ: It's a green spiral. That's your answer about the symbolism.

NF: It is one response, I could develop others.

CJ: But that, in a way, justifies the building. In other words, in terms of public symbolism there has to be a content that is worthy of being expressed, of being explicit.

### Fame and competitions

CJ: But let's come back to this question of fame versus celebrity, longevity. You are building for the long term, but what about other architects?

NF: Last year I went to the 25th anniversary of the Willis Faber Building and took a photograph, unconsciously, from exactly where I had before. I was staggered to find the two were almost identical except that one had typewriters and the other had word processors. I had become involved with students in the university at Singapore, and they were playing with typewriters as art objects that were almost excavated from the past. They'd never seen anybody actually use a typewriter. For that Willis Faber anniversary they had all the past players including two chairmen. One of them said, 'Norman had this crazy idea about change and designing for change. We were all very patient, it didn't seem to cost us anything to indulge him. But he was absolutely right. Never in our wildest dreams did we imagine that the technology would change and our competitors would have to pull down their buildings and build new ones'. In the same way the Hongkong Bank might boast that it is the only high-risk bank headquarters in the world, to their knowledge, where they have been able to put in a dealers' floor later on, because the building didn't have a central core. I think that if a building is able to adapt, then it will survive. If it doesn't, it will just fall by the wayside.

CJ: You're displacing the question though. I'm talking about the fame of an architect rather than just the longevity of a building. There's a way in which Bramante's fame has lasted, although he was called 'Bramante ruinante', because a lot of his buildings fell into ruins.

NF: No!

CJ: Yes. At the time even, and they were the words of his enemies.

NF: How do you find all this out? You're extraordinary!

CJ: I don't know – just part of architectural history. Why I am interested in this question is the pressures fame puts on you and other professional architects. If, for instance, you disappear from the front page in the modern world, you're dead. Amnesia and modernism are directly connected because of the business cycle, continual change, and the constant need to appear new. People, under these pressures of the new, forget about you, and therefore you lose potential clients and so on …You have a very big practice. You always have to be in the public eye.

NF: I don't agree – all buildings are in the public eye. Some of our most important commissions are from those who come back a second or third time over many years or from those new potential clients who examine the performance of buildings that we might have completed a long time ago. But of course it is also true

Willis Faber and Dumas Building, Ipswich, 1970–4. This building for an East Anglia-based insurance company sealed Foster's reputation in the early 70s. The building's plan responds ingeniously to the medieval street pattern of Ipswich by being low and deep. At it perimeter, a necklace of columns flow, in Lord Foster's words, to the edge of the site 'like a pancake in a pan', thus filling and curving around the ancient street plan. Much attention was paid inside to the needs of the office as a properly integrated and democratic workplace. With two floors of open plan offices, the interior can be clearly viewed from the central escalators.

Above left
Exterior view at night of the Willis Faber and Dumas Building, Ipswich.

Above right
Interior view of the escalators in the Willis Faber and Dumas Building, Ipswich.

that architecture and architects as a profession have a higher profile today than, say, 30 years ago.

CJ: On the question of "profiles" …

NF: There is a contradiction – the reality is that it is becoming increasingly difficult for a single group, let alone an individual, to steer the destiny of a project. Many talented individuals from related professions are involved regardless of whether they are credited. As buildings, and the infrastructure that binds them together, become even more complex it becomes increasingly difficult to sustain any relatively single-minded design initiative. One tendency is the concept of individual creativity and accountability combined with the larger groups who are able to invest in specialised technology, which is increasingly being demanded by all the parties in large construction projects. I am not talking about a relatively simple project like a museum, but large public infrastructure. In America you see this tendency in the combination of firms behind projects.

CJ: I think the subject of fame/celebrity is of interest, partly because it's so powerful and also such a taboo. In other words, it's very unclear how the systems of fame and celebrity work today, but an architect and designer has to acknowledge them either one way or another – keep their name in front of the public and their reputation good – there's no question. Certainly one can see this with upcoming practices, or an old hand at fame/celebrity, Philippe Starck: they kill to get interviews, they kill to have their name out there, because that's the main way they can get work. Like actors. I don't think that's your

experience, historically.

NF: Don't forget that there is also the tradition of anonymous competitions.

CJ: Really? Well, let's unpack that idea. So you're saying that through competitions, and not through covert advertising and reputation, you've made your way in the world. That's what you're basically saying.

NF: I am trying to be analytical, you have mentioned a number of buildings such as…

CJ: Gateshead, Glasgow, Commerzbank.

NF: Commerzbank, like the Reichstag, was an anonymous competition!

CJ: You know the famous story of the opera house in Paris?

NF: I do indeed.

CJ: Where the judges thought they were getting Richard Meier?

NF: Yes but coming back to your earlier point, I think you can overplay the media bit – I know that for every occasional interview that we give, there are scores that we routinely turn down.

CJ: So you're saying that the work speaks for itself.

NF: In the end it has to.

CJ: You're saying that fame comes as a by-product; it's not either a fore-product or something that you seek; it is simply a consequence of what you're doing. I think, of course, that's the classic position – 'classic' in the sense of tradition. Architects have always claimed not to be seeking fame, except the one that Vitruvius mentioned, who tells you how to get the job. But having said that, of course you know that your name is out there through thousands of articles and publications on you, so you don't have to promote yourself. Frank Lloyd Wright said, when he was asked about the Johnson Wax Building, that he wanted to send them a bill for seven million dollars' worth of advertisement, because of all the buzz

in the architectural press and popular magazines. *Time* magazine put him on the cover, and said it was a most famous building (which it instantly was by being so proclaimed). So he didn't need what the other poor, struggling architects are desperately trying to get – that is to say good copy in a mass circulation weekly. He was getting it from critics. I understand that this is the classic position, and I'm sure that you're right, Norman. I would not accuse you of being other than what you say. But aside from that there is this system of patronage, your knighthood, your being made a Lord, and all of that, which is extremely important within the system, and people – that is, other architects and the public – can't see how that happens. I wonder if you can shed some light on that.

NF: I can't shed any light on it.

CJ: Are you asked if X or Y should get a knighthood? Are your opinions canvassed?

NF: No, not at all.

CJ: Hmmm. Do you feel that architectural culture – because this is what it comes to – is functioning well in this country in its distribution of jobs, patronage and fame? I would say that, for instance, 40 years ago it was functioning extremely badly, that the worst architects were getting the best jobs, and therefore it had broken down. Today it has got better.

NF: I think it's day and night. It was awful in the past. There's no comparison. Now it's far more transparent, it's more accountable.

CJ: And better architects are getting better work too.

NF: Yes, which is terrific.

CJ: It's unbelievable over the last 10 years, don't you think?

NF: It's fantastic, yes. And I'd rephrase what you're saying to make the point that it is long overdue in this country, following a European model where there is a far greater, healthier interest in architecture. The attitude has always been here in the general environment, although I don't think it's been as well promoted as it could have been by those who represent the interests of the public. I remember the dialogue with the community in public meetings when we were designing the Hammersmith Centre in the 1970s. There was even a public petition in favour of the project. I can think of other examples, like Stansted, and talking to the locals there at the time of the public enquiry. So at a grass-roots level there has always been a keen interest in architecture, but it has not been communicated as well as it should have been by the media. But things have changed, why? Whether it's the inspired examples from outside these shores, whether it's a change in the climate, whether it's a change in the government, whether it's the liberation of public funds through the Lottery, – whatever the combination of factors, things have changed. There is healthier, wider, greater debate; more interest; you can open a weekend newspaper and find the subject up front. You couldn't do that before. And there are competitions galore.

CJ: So architectural culture has improved, comparatively. Last question. On this chart of the years 1900 to 2000 there are 450 architects, 100 trends – and by 'trends' I mean things like plastics, internet, mobile homes, the Second World War (as a trend – horrible!) – and there are 60 'isms' that became 'wasms', like Brutalism, Metabolism, Purism and all the other isms. It means that at any one time there are four isms, five trends and 100 architects who are competing on a world level (this is global architecture). I would argue, as a critic, that what I'm writing about, what I'm showing

This page
Commerzbank Headquarters,
Frankfurt, 1991–7. Foster's
office won the job through an
anonymous competition entry.

Opposite
The final section of Charles
Jencks's diagram that maps
the architects movements of
the previous century, as
discussed on the previous and
opposite page.

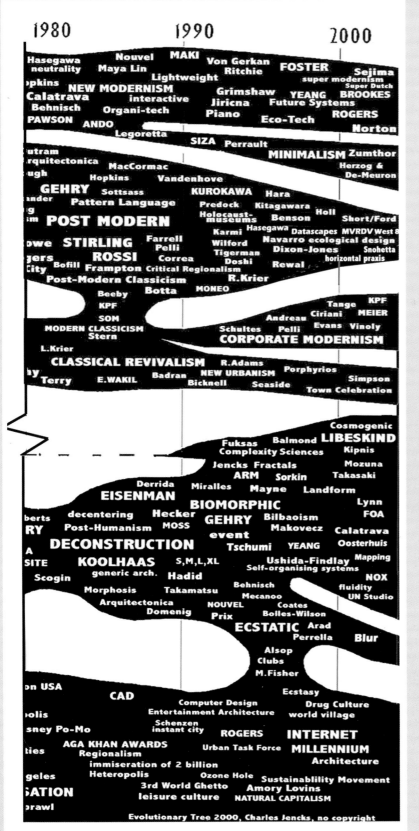

1980    1990    2000

Evolutionary Tree 2000, Charles Jencks, no copyright

here, is fame in a deep sense – in other words, something that's important, lasting and has quality. I see my job as a critic as lifting up the ones I think are good and knocking the ones I think are bad. Why else be a critic? Why waste your time? But I have to say that if you look at the century as a whole, it's been very turbulent. That's why all these blobs pulsate with such angst. Le Corbusier, who I think was arguably the greatest architect of the last century, led it by changing every ten years or so. It's what is called 'the ten-year rule'; that's an incredible amount of change, that means changing, like Picasso did, five times in his life. Now, you have started to change too. Perhaps twice or three times in the past, generically, and with the computer now you are beginning to open up a new kind of grammar of design, of which Swiss Re and Gateshead are examples.

Do you think there is a competition for leadership? Does the global situation spur change, or would you argue, as the cognitive scientist Howard Gardner suggests about the ten year rule, that it comes from the internal psychology of the person? Does the changing outside world force you to change your assumptions, or does your creative dynamic come from within?

NF: It's easier for somebody from outside to speculate about how individuals and groups evolve. For me, change comes genuinely from within, but it has to be responsive to the changing needs which generate architecture in the first place.

CJ: But you do compete. You will be in the final selection lists with the big 10: there are always the usual suspects. That's what my diagram shows: 'round up the usual suspects'.

NF: It's true, that there are some patterns.

CJ: You are highly competitive, Norman. If I see you in a competition, I know you're in there to win.

NF: Do you not think that we are also competing against ourselves? Last Sunday I joined the Engadine ski marathon – 42.5 kilometres through Swiss forests, villages and across frozen lakes – along with 13,000 other competitors. We all had our individual goals – different ideas of victory. I set out to beat three hours – and made it by 37 seconds!

CJ: It's the classic answer of the head of Bryanston School and his advice to pupils: 'Don't worry about others – just try to beat your own best at golf.'

NF: But when you say it's the classic answer, I can only give you the ...

CJ: Your view.

NF: Yes.

CJ: Of course. When I say that I don't mean to belittle it at all. In fact I think it would be my answer anyway! Δ

# It is not that difficult to become famous if you really want to:

## Sean Griffiths of FAT in Conversation with Torsten Schmiedeknecht

Sean Griffiths is the only remaining founding member of FAT – Fashion Architecture Taste – the multidisciplinary London-based practice known for its unconventional approach to architecture and its preference for the representational over the abstract. Having been in the public eye for a number of years, Griffiths airs his thoughts on fame to guest-editor Torsten Schmiedeknecht. Understanding architecture in the context of fashion and branding, Griffiths explains from where FAT draw their inspiration and their intention that each project should open possibilities for multiple readings.

Torsten Schmiedeknecht: The *∆ Fame and Architecture* is, among other issues concerned with two systems of fame: fame within the architectural community and fame within society. Are FAT operating on the fringe of both these systems?

Sean Griffiths: Yes. There are two interesting issues here regarding the 21st century vision of what fame is. Architects have always been famous: Palladio was famous and so was Michelangelo. This obviously has an effect on the kind of buildings that are being produced and this has always been the case. What is probably more interesting for us is the relationship between architecture and a culture of celebrity in a much wider sense. We are interested in architecture and culture rather than architecture amidst other architecture. It is really about architecture and its relationship to a society that buys god knows how many copies of *Hello Magazine* or architecture and its relationship

to a society in which as religious icons you get David Beckham and Posh Spice. It links back to Andy Warhol and the fifteen minutes of fame. The fifteen minutes are also suggestive of changing fashions – something that is negated within architecture and not being talked about. We embrace and recognise this as a factor within architectural production: the cycles of fashion and the effect it has on the built environment in quite a direct way.

So the question of taste is a very central part of everything we do and despite the denial by a lot of architects of the impact that fashion and fame have on architecture we are trying to reference these things and to acknowledge their influence in our work.

Many architects deny that they are actively playing the fame game and they seem to promote the idea that their careers are solely built on their architectural merits. But it is well known that most of the American and British superstars come from comfortable backgrounds – both financially and regarding their networking potential. The French

sociologist Pierre Bourdieu claims that architecture always has to be seen in the context of the society which allows it to be built and thus that there is no such thing as inherently great architecture.

I would not necessarily agree with Bourdieu on those particular points. I don't think that there is anybody who would deny that Palladio was a great architect and that he was head and shoulders above a lot of what else was produced at that time. Regarding your first point about contemporary architects not acknowledging the bearing their media profile has on the way that their work is seen, I think this is simply ludicrous.

**Did you want to become famous when you were a student? What do you think it is that drives us and makes us to want to become recognised and see our names in print?**

I suppose if I am honest: yes, I wanted to become famous! There are obvious reasons like recognition of your work that give you a certain sense of satisfaction. The main reason of why I would want to become famous is because it is a valuable marketing tool. Through getting our work published in the last few years we have now started to reap some benefits and have been approached by people who think that what we are doing is interesting. There are of course other nice little side effects and perks. You go off and give a little lecture in Europe and I don't suppose that there are many people who would find giving a lecture particularly discomforting – seeing that there are people who come to listen to you and are curious about what you are doing. But the main issue of fame for us is purely marketing.

It goes with the idea of branding. Look at

people like Gehry, Koolhaas and Hadid: properly famous people who are taken on to do what they do. They are a kind of brand, which becomes associated with whoever is commissioning them. Frank Gehry is now forever going to be linked to the Guggenheim. Now he is doing one in New York that seems to me to be exactly the same as the one in Bilbao. That is where fame becomes rather boring. Zaha Hadid's work becomes instantly recognisable – however anonymous a competition might be – so it's really about choosing a brand.

**Brands are marketed and advertised through imagery, which is also the driving force behind your work. What is the importance of space and its creation and the relationship between space and place for you?**

The relationship between image and space is an enormously complex one. Architecture increasingly operates in two spheres: the 'real' – which is obviously to do with using and experiencing buildings – and the world of images. Architectural space is not a neutral thing. It is affected by its imagery. The imagery is part of how people read space and how it works in a symbolic way.

Another reason why we are interested in the image is because in our culture it is becoming more dominant. One of the things we have observed in advertising in the UK in the last ten years is the incredible development of the level of visual sophistication. Our culture has become more visually sophisticated and is interested in the kind of images that have symbolic meaning in the same way as Posh and Becks have. We are interested in representational architecture and we find abstraction very boring because it locks the subject into its relationship with the history of architecture rather than perhaps expanding and reflecting on some other things.

**When people come and see your projects, do you desire for them to gain an understanding of what's going on and to be able to read it?**

Opposite left
Photo of Sean Griffiths.

Opposite right
FAT, street elevation of house on Garner Street, London, 1999-2001.

Above left
FAT, Sitooterie Pavilion, Belsay Hall, Northumberland, 2000.

Above right
FAT, axonometric of house on Garner Street, London, 1999-2001.

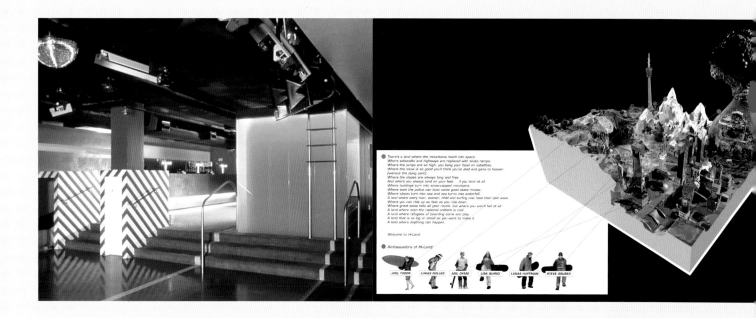

Our work makes references to 'high' architecture but it also has readings that are accessible to others. A tactic we use is to take something that is very familiar and to then manipulate it in a way that gives it a high art reading. Both readings can exist at the same time and thus the work can be related to other forms of architecture but someone who is not an architect can also enjoy it. One example of that was the Brunel Rooms nightclub in Swindon. The people who were going to use the nightclub had a very sophisticated notion of the club culture that they were involved in. They were essentially very young and these kids go out to have a great time and not to stand in reverence in front of wonderful architecture. The architecture was only going to play a small part in their experience of a night out. The quality of the DJ or whether you got off with someone that night or what kind of drugs you took was always going to be more important. So the idea was really to try and intensify the experience for these people. We created snippets of other familiar images and spaces in order to give the space both readings – high art and low art.

Architecture itself is a lot more about branding now than it ever used to be. The boundaries between the brand image and high art seem to be dissolving – for better or for worse – which becomes evident in the work of people like Koolhaas and it links back to what I said earlier about the increasing level of visual sophistication in our culture.

**This is interesting because one finds a lot of students, even in 4th and 5th year struggling to understand the relationship between space and image. There always seems to be this distinction between the so-called real and the so-called artificial. It is hilarious. Their whole behaviour and identity is so much determined by what they absorb through what ever media and yet they refuse to accept the media as a very real and tangible part of reality and thus as a valid tool for architectural production.**

The use of the media as a means to realise and market work and ideas in some form is something that is recognised by a lot of people. David Greene – one of our teachers – and Archigram realised this essential relationship between architecture and the media and subsequently produced their work as a magazine. FAT also started as the intention to make a magazine which unfortunately never got off the ground because what was required of a magazine in the 1990s was relatively sophisticated as a product and we couldn't quite do what Archigram had done which was essentially cut and paste with a pen, paper and a copier. Nevertheless the relationship between our work and its presentation in other forms than the built reality is certainly very important. We did this project for Diesel Jeans where they wanted the invention of a land were you could do anything, an image of an urban environment which was subsequently realised in form of a big model which was then used for an advertising shoot for a series of extreme sportswear products. It was urbanism derived from branding and contained a series of associations of a city in which you could do anything. Similar to what Tschumi was talking about: hang gliding in the lift shaft etc. It was a completely imaginary urban environment with mountain ranges and surf waves and so on. We are getting increasingly more things like that to do, which interest us because the amount of advertising and media in the city is increasing all the time. We are coming from a branding and advertising angle and what

we are doing has nothing to do with architectural formalism but it is to do with imagery and symbolism and association to a particular product.

About two years ago Peter Zumthor gave a lecture at the RIBA in which he refused to show slides of his buildings – apart from one – and instead gave a talk about his idea of beauty which he illustrated with slides of monochrome squares. He denied the power of the mediated experience, arguing that his buildings could only be understood on location as it were. Considering that he is one of the most published contemporary architects I was asking myself at the time: doesn't he watch TV, doesn't he look at magazines.

That is absolutely symptomatic of the way that architects think about architecture in relation to site and there often is only one authentic reading which is the architect's own reading. In my view that's total nonsense. Is it 35 years since Robert Venturi talked about 'both and' rather than 'either or'? Zumthor's reading of his buildings is only one valid reading but he has to acknowledge that there are other valid ones through magazines and images and so on. And all these readings can only add to what the building has to offer so they are making it better rather than worse. It is a very strange attitude in architecture that you can somehow miraculously isolate architecture so that it can never be contaminated by the city, by culture. But architecture only becomes interesting at that point when it becomes contaminated by the culture. One of the reasons why I didn't see Zumthor's lecture was because

I am absolutely bored to tears by that argument. As an architect you always have to remember that you are only participating in the built environment.

Our office project for Kessels Kramer for instance. We could have gone in there with a photographer when it was still empty and do the obvious architect's photographs. But in fact, once they had filled the space it became a lot more exiting, a bit like a flea market. They often send us photographs and it illustrates how different the place can look and we think that's great. The fact that our projects are being appropriated is the most exiting thing to us.

My last question is regarding your manual of *How to become a famous architect*.[1] Does it bare autobiographical links? Do you accept that there is such a thing as the fame game?

There are obviously links but it is also a bit tongue in cheek. It is a comment on how you develop something which is considered to be interesting and ways in which certain authorities can be built. With regards to us acknowledging certain rules of the fame game: being in London helps a lot. You get to meet the various editors and most journalists are actually very lazy and don't venture out beyond London. They might go to Bilbao, but not to Manchester or Liverpool. It is not that difficult to get your work published if you really want to. ∆

Background
FAT, courtyard elevation of house on Garner Street, London, 1999–2001.

Notes
1. The guide of *How to become a famous architect* is accessible on FAT's website on www.fat.co.uk/howto/

# High-Tech
## Knights

'Social lions at home, feted abroad' the High-Tech architects have gained themselves an eminent position in British society, as reflected in the last decade's crop of architectural knighthoods. Is the presence of architects in the Queen's Honours List an anomaly of the past ten years or part of a greater tradition? Jeremy Melvin shows how the emphasis on honours has shifted over the 20th century from those involved in architectural publishing or public service to individual signature architects. Melvin also asks how architects fare in comparison to other professions and exactly what the impact of the new Prime Minister's Better Public Building award might be on the present system of honours.

A palpable sense of anticipation went round the editorial offices of the weekly architectural periodicals one Friday afternoon in June 1990. Correspondents from national newspapers were on the phone asking for information. They had seen early, embargoed copies of the Queen's Birthday Honours List, to be published the following day and spotted, among the new knights, one Foster, Norman Robert, 'for services to architecture'. It seemed that modern architecture, after six years of royalist bombardment, was on the verge of rehabilitation. We already knew that Foster was scheduled to teach at the Prince of Wales' summer school that year, but this was in a different league altogether. 'Was he the only knighted architect?', the august journalists wanted to know. The more knowledgeable among them might have added 'since Christopher Wren' or maybe 'Edwin Lutyens' or even, for those with more recherché tastes and esoteric knowledge, 'since Basil Spence'.

The answer was that there were actually numerous knighted architects. But they were not, on the whole, those whose names tripped off the tongue as leaders of the profession. Perhaps the most noted designer among them, Denys Lasdun, was going through a passing phase of not using his title in some vague protest against Prince Charles' comments on the National Theatre. Sir Philip Powell was moving towards retirement. And the most recent additions to their ranks were architects who were noted for their abilities in committee than at the drawing board: Sir Bernard Feilden, saviour of numerous cathedrals; Sir Alex Gordon, holder of seats on myriad construction industry working groups; RMJM's Sir Andrew Derbyshire, who spawned *The Architect and His Office* in the early 1960s, and Hillingdon Town Hall during the following decade. Another identifiable group comprised Sir John Summerson and Sir James Richards, prominent as writers rather than designers – neatly ironic since 'knighted architect' was a pejorative term coined in their youth to describe the crusty old Lutyenses, Richardsons, Bakers and Blomfields. Adding the not-so-long-deceased Sir Osbert Lancaster, Sir John Betjeman and Sir Nikolaus Pevsner though, suggested that proximity to architectural publishing in the fabulous 1930s was a surer route to knighthood than practising High Tech in the 1980s.

Foster's knighthood exploded that assumption, and brought the honours system to the heart of the architectural avant-garde. Similar awards in the next two years to Richard Rogers and Jim Stirling – who was tragically to die within days – seemed to bring architecture to the heart of the honours system and, therefore, in the peculiar constitution of British society, to the centre stage of social eminence. It's axiomatic that gossip columnists need a tag to identify their subject; 'heiress' or 'old Etonian' will do, but nothing beats a proper handle. Possessing a real, tangible title helped to open the door to more vicarious and transitory notions of fame. 1990, it will be remembered, was also the year that *Hello!* became embedded in national consciousness, and soft-focus treatment of the socially eminent entered popular consumer fare. Much else fell into place: Foster, the ultimate loft-dweller, just before it became really fashionable; Rogers, partner in one of the most fashionable eateries that helped eating to become a fashion statement. It's hard to remember, more than a decade on, how uncertain it was that these trends would succeed, at the beginning of the nineties before the grey dawn of John Major lifted the dark night of Thatcherism. It is a compliment to the people who dish out knighthoods that they recognised these trends before they became established, and were able to add further honours in the shape of peerages for Foster and Rogers, knighthoods to Michael Hopkins and Colin Stansfield Smith and a CBE to Nick Grimshaw to confirm the bonds between High Tech and the Establishment. Include Sir Colin St John (Sandy) Wilson, Sir Jeremy Dixon and Sir Richard MacCormac, and the avant-garde architectural honours overwhelmingly outweigh the greyer knights of the last decade: Chateau Fergiana designer Sir James Dunbar Nasmith and Sir William Whitfield.

Opposite
Richard Rogers, with his wife Ruth, and sons Zad (left) and Roo (right) at Buckingham Palace after he was knighted on 7 November 1991 by the Queen for Services to Architecture.

Top
RIBA president Frank Duffy shows gentlemanly politesse while presenting the Royal Gold Medal to Michael and Patty Hopkins in 1994. The following year Hopkins received a knighthood, while that year's Gold Medal laureate, Colin Rowe, confessed that he had considered subjecting Duffy to the "full Latino routine of huggin' an' rubbin' and kissin'", before decorum reasserted itself. Duffy himself was to be appointed a CBE after his presidency ended in 1995.

In reality, architects have never had it so good as far as knighthoods are concerned, and CBES are ten a penny. Representation in the House of Lords, the ultimate peak of the honours system, is less positive. True, there are two architect peers, but that is not unprecedented: Lords Llewelyn-Davies and Holford sat at the same time, uncannily one a Labour working peer and the other ennobled for services to architecture. And the cull of hereditaries removed at least four architects: the duke of Gloucester, Viscount Esher (PPRIBA), and Lords Cunliffe and Hankey, the latter known to the cognoscenti as 'Tissue'. There had been hereditary peer architects in the past, notably the late duke of Wellington (who had practiced as Lord Gerald Wellesley), the late Lord Phillimore, remodeller of many a country house to suit the postwar dearth of servants, and the late Lord Mottistone, partner in Seeley and Paget, fashionable *décorateurs* of

but worthy architects of large public buildings. Nash was reputedly offered a baronetcy but it was never confirmed. If it had been, he would have been the first architect to be given (rather than to have inherited) a hereditary title, but as the supposedly gay husband of one of the Prince of Wales' mistresses, there may have been the ulterior motive of an elder son having something to inherit.

Only in the 20th century did any architects receive hereditary honours – and these were mere baronetcies (the style is to be Sir somebody something and does not carry a seat in the House of Lords). The names of the two recipients are hardly at the forefront of architectural history. They are Sir TG Jackson, architect of much of late Victorian Oxford, and Sir Alfred Bossom, a long-serving Conservative Member of Parliament who was also the first architect to receive a life peerage. Neither have architect descendants. Living architects who have inherited baronetcies include Sir Thomas Croft, while Sir Martyn Beckett died recently.

In reality, architects have never had it so good as far as knighthoods are concerned

the 1930s. Back in the early 18th century, there was the earl of Burlington, with an ageing but still active Sir Christopher Wren and the rambunctious Sir John Vanburgh.

It was Wren who paved the way for architects to receive knighthoods. His origins – son of a dean of Windsor, nephew of a bishop, educated at Westminster and Oxford where he became a professor – made the award rather easier than if he had come from an artisanal family. Even so, he hardly opened the floodgates. Vanburgh's honour came more from his position as a herald than his architectural achievements, and the next noted knights only come at the end of the 18th century: Sir William Chambers and Sir Robert Taylor. Both had sizeable country house practices, and Taylor's connection to the Bank of England forged an important connection with business. In the next generation this stood Sir John Soane in good stead when he designed the bank's building, though his knighthood came relatively late (perhaps his artisanal background stood against him); Robert Smirke foreshadowed the idea of knighting dull

By the date of Bossom's peerage (1959), few of the old 'knighted architects' of the 1930s were left and the modernists had started to make their mark. Summerson was knighted in 1957, but by then was less an advocate of modernism than an erudite historian. FRS Yorke received a CBE days before he died in 1962 and honours began to accrue to his contemporaries: Basil Spence, the Johnson Marshall brothers, Stirrat and Percy, Casson knighted as early as 1951 for the Festival of Britain, Gibberd, Leslie Martin. Indeed there was a point where being the London County Council's or the Greater London Council's chief architect almost guaranteed a knighthood: Roger Walters, knighted in 1971 while in that position, is now the senior architectural knight. Contrary to popular belief, the position of president of the RIBA never carried an automatic knighthood. Before MacCormac the only other living knighted PPRIBA is Peter Shepheard, president in the early 1970s.

Given this proliferation of architectural honours – numerous civil servants and even some commercial architects have received CBES – there have to be some further distinctions. One might be to calibrate the state honours system with specifically architectural awards. Foster, Rogers and Stirling all received the RIBA's gold medal some time before their knighthoods; for Hopkins, the gap was just one year. And it is very rare for a knighthood to precede receipt of the gold mMedal. International honours give a more mixed signal. Foster has added the Praemium Imperiale, the Pritzker Prize and the AIA's gold medal since his knighthood; Rogers has added the Praemium Imperiale while Stirling won the Pritzker and Praemium Imperiale before he was knighted.

Another measure is prestigious honours that are awarded by the state, but which do not carry a title: admission to the Companions of Honour and the Order of Merit. Philip Powell is a CH – as were Casson, Lasdun and Summerson. But only five architects have been admitted to the Order of Merit, a very serious honour limited to only 24

Medical Council and the Regius Professorship at Oxford bringing one of the latter almost automatically. Knighthoods abounded then, as they still do now. But somehow they didn't have quite the same style or eminence as the present crop of honoured architects: social lions at home, feted abroad, their skill and achievements acknowledged through the state honours system as through international architectural awards.

Mr Blair is seeking to bring his own brand of order to the chaos of contemporary architectural honours. February 2001 saw the launch of the Prime Minister's Better Public Building award, which grew out of CABE's Better Public Buildings document published in 2000. As an initiative specifically to promote architecture in the public sector (though that is not straightforward to define), it is an intersection between recognition of a contribution to public service and architectural quality – the latter also not easy to define. Predictably, the definition of quality that seems to have been adopted

Perhaps, in the curious limbo between a class-based honours system and the meritocratic dream of Mr Anthony Blair, where the void is filled by media speculation, architecture and honours have found temporary solace. Both, after all, seek to impose order on chaos

holders at any one time, which ranks with the Victoria Cross and Knight of the Garter in prestige. One of these was not even honoured for services to architecture: he was a certain Thomas Hardy. The others were Lutyens, Giles Gilbert Scott, Spence and, of course, Foster, probably the most honoured architect in history.

A final way of calibrating architectural honours is a comparison with other professions. The Church of England and the Bar has privileged representation, with the Law Lords and 21 bishops sitting in the House of Lords. High Court judges additionally receive automatic knighthoods, but other lawyers are curiously under-represented except for those who seek advancement through politics. Accountants and surveyors also seem to miss out, with a smaller proportion receiving honours than architects; teachers (apart from very senior university staff) and nurses have a pretty bad deal. Doctors are different. In the days of hereditary honours several were awarded peerages and many received baronetcies, with some positions such as chair of the General

plays to government shibboleths and is an extension of the British Construction Industry awards rather than of, say, the RIBA's. The award will mark a collective achievement rather than that of an individual, and it measures 'value' and client satisfaction as well as design. Who knows – might it be Blair's blueprint for an exciting new, modernised honours system? If so, architecture really would be leading public policy.

Perhaps, in the curious limbo between a class-based honours system and the meritocratic dream of Mr Anthony Blair, where the void is filled by media speculation, architecture and honours have found temporary solace. Both, after all, seek to impose order on chaos.

Jeremy Melvin studied architecture and history of architecture at the Bartlett, UCL. He contributes to various publications (including AD Technical Studies); has published Young British Architects, and is shortly to publish a monograph on FRS Yorke; teaches at South bank University; and is a member of the Academy Forum and the International Committee of the Friends of the Viipuri Library.

# Breaking all taboos

John Outram in Conversation with Helen Castle

Indifferent to the vicissitudes and vacillations of fashion, John Outram is unstinting in his pursuit of his own architectural vision. Experience and a conviction in his own ideas have made him both aware of as well as inured to the peaks and troughs of celebrity. In an interview with Helen Castle, Editor of *Architectural Design*, John Outram casts some valuable insights into fame and celebrity, describing with some precision exactly how signature architecture has its roots in the American building industry.

John Outram has ridden high on the intoxicating wave of renown, having come to prominence in the 1980s under post-modernism. When in 1988, he completed the Storm Water Pumping Station on the Isle of Dogs, narrative and its readings were *de rigueur;* he was widely lauded for the building's iconography and its complex depictions of mythologies. In 1991 his contribution to architecture was acknowledged by the establishment when he was chosen to represent Britain at the Venice Biennale alongside the late James Stirling, Lord Foster, Lord Rogers, Nicholas Grimshaw and Sir Michael Hopkins. In the last ten years, Outram has completed some major commissions, including the Judge Institute of Management Studies, Cambridge, 1995; Duncan Hall, the Computational Research Engineering Faculty for Rice University in Houston, Texas, 1997; and a major addition to the 16th-century town hall in the Groenmarkt, The Hague, 1999. By his own omission, however, he has been tainted by the label of post-modernism and rejected by fashion-orientated taste, which in the early 90s shifted away from the figurative and the decorative back towards modernism and reductivism.

**Helen Castle: Has the recent shift in architectural fashion affected the way you gain commissions? You have said that you don't expect anything of Europe.[1] Ironically perhaps, because you've fairly recently completed the Groenmarkt in The Hague and you have just been commissioned to execute a 'new lifestyle' project for Bouwfonds, the largest house builders in The Netherlands.**

John Outram: Yes, one is always surprised.

**HC: Do you think it may be also that you're going to come back with a vengeance?**

JO: Well, it's given me time ... as my wife puts it, God gave me time to think. We've always had enough work. We've normally had a succession of rather large projects, but of late we've had quite a few small projects. The 'Haverleij Castle' concept, invented by Sjoerd Soeters, is our first large project for two or three years. I like large projects, because my architecture has developed from an urbanistic base. I think the fashion cycle is powered by the Oedipal drive. Every generation wants to kill its fathers, especially nowadays, because the fathers live for so long. It must be very oppressive for a student to have people like Foster and Rogers all being frightfully avant-garde. What is a young man supposed to do? In my day, you see, we were up against a bunch of clearly super-annuated fuddy-duddies.

The thing that always interferes with our ability to land the final commission has been aptly defined by Michael Graves. He actually said to one of our potential clients, 'You've got to be careful with Outram; he's an architect who doesn't know when to stop.' I think this is it, you see: we start where everybody else stops. We start with iconography and ornament increasingly. We start where the taboo stops other people.[2]

My career has gone through two cycles. The first jobs we did were for friends and relations – people we knew, who didn't know anything about architecture and didn't know anything about what we'd done, because we hadn't done anything. Once we'd done our first cycle of work, nobody would employ us. People used to come and look at our work and clearly wanted a glass box with a Porsche outside, because that's what a successful entrepreneur wanted. We did strange vast columns with flaming capitals, and huge cornices and things like that. Our second wind was when we were picked up during the post-modernist period, by big clients and developers like Stuart Lipton. We were interviewed for the National Gallery extension, which again we were too colourful to get.

**HC: You've just continued with your own approach.**

JO: I remember I once met Peter Murray at the RIBA, and he said I was the only architect he knew who was totally careless of the opinion of his peer group. He also said that I was one of the few architects whose buildings looked exactly like their drawings! I thought the latter remark was very curious, because I thought to myself, 'well, why bother to do drawings, if the building doesn't come out like them?' But I know what he meant. What he meant was, you did the drawing and somebody took it away from you and screwed it up. That I never allowed to happen. I would rather resign the project, which at Battersea I did – £500-million worth. I gave it back to them, because they refused to let me dominate the drawing. They said, 'The people in Vegas want something changed; they have an illustrator who will change it.' That was the breaking point.

**HC: On your website, there is a very interesting piece written by you on Duncan Hall. In it you describe the prejudice that the architectural faculty at Rice University exercised against you and your building, this was in spite of its popularity with the university as a whole and the general public. You describe the architectural department as feeling that Duncan Hall was somehow 'wrong', in a 'narrowly "architectural" sense of what is moral and ethical'. This consensus among architectural academia of what is right or wrong or 'in' or 'out' pervades the profession and both the architectural press and, in turn, the national media. It can be decisive.**

JO: The first time I met this cult of fame was when I gave a lecture to Plymouth School of Architecture in 1984. The students kept coming up to me afterwards,

Opposite
John Outram at 'The Victorians' exhibition that he designed for the Victoria and Albert Museum in 2001.

Above top
John Outram on the September 1987 issue of *Blueprint.*

Above bottom
John Outram as a pilot during his national service.

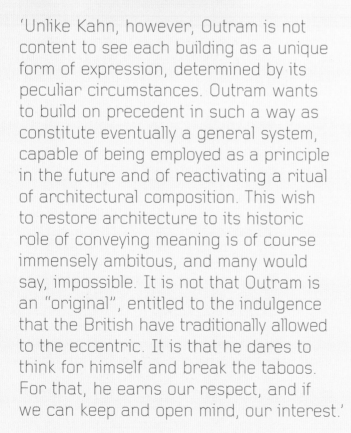

'Unlike Kahn, however, Outram is not content to see each building as a unique form of expression, determined by its peculiar circumstances. Outram wants to build on precedent in such a way as constitute eventually a general system, capable of being employed as a principle in the future and of reactivating a ritual of architectural composition. This wish to restore architecture to its historic role of conveying meaning is of course immensely ambitous, and many would say, impossible. It is not that Outram is an "original", entitled to the indulgence that the British have traditionally allowed to the eccentric. It is that he dares to think for himself and break the taboos. For that, he earns our respect, and if we can keep and open mind, our interest.'

Bob Maxwell, Emeritus professor of Architecture, Columbia University, writing about the Judge Institute in *Architecture Today*, November 1995.

and I noticed they were rather more ignorant than I had met before. They didn't know anything about Corbusier or Mies van der Rohe or anything really, but what they wanted to know was how to become famous. I thought this was very odd – Adrian Gale was the school head. I asked him, 'What is it with your students? They keep asking me how to become famous. Well, I can't tell them.'

**HC: I wondered whether you thought this alliance between architectural academia and the media were creating pop stars or soaps stars, or they were being king-makers. Do you think they're peddling celebrity or fame really?**

JO: It's a complicated question. It does seem to have originated in America, and there are good technical reasons to do with the licensing laws. Each state tends to restrict architectural work to their own licensees. If a client wants another architect, they have to import them from another state.

It is probably less local now than it was a few years ago. Certainly in Houston, Gerald Heinz, a famous developer – who has now left, and is living in London's Notting Hill, having built everything the city will ever need for the next 40 years – developed the idea of the signature architect. By bringing in a named architect on a skyscraper, he realised you could increase its saleability.

Heinz brought in people like Johnson. Then the University picked up on the idea. The chairwoman of the University was a friend of Heinz, and he was project manager of a Rice University project, and so learnt

how to handle the 'design architect' strategy. American architects used to be just like architects used to be here. They did all the working drawings. When I worked in America, though, I found that there is no middle to the building industry.

There are a lot of very expensive houses – a $6 million house is nothing – and they keep all the craft firms going. A lot of architects cut their teeth on that – building an expensive house for a relation. Americans will also build a succession of homes; it's part of the moral imperative of being a good consumer: you build a house, then move and build another house. It keeps the ceremony going like nothing else. The same craftsmen also work on the elevator lobbies of the skyscrapers. Then there's Sweets catalogue, which is about two metres long, and you just build buildings over the telephone. Your pen never touches the paper. There's this incredible culture of ...

**HC: Off the peg.**

JO: Yes, the contractor is king. The American building worker is directly descended from the Frontiersman. I call him the 'heroic handyman'. He wears a gun-belt of handtools. He thinks of himself as shooting and skinning an animal, building a house, doing the plumbing and wiring and building the furniture. He has a heroic dimension.

When I first worked on a building site, back in the 50s, the British workers turned up in torn suits. They were 'fallen Gentlemen'. They were resentful. When an American building worker says, 'I'll call on Tuesday' he is not sumbitting to your authority. He is doing you a favour. The Americans developed mass production because they were short of labour. The Europeans developed offsite production because siteworkers went on strike. Yet the American builder is highly Unionised. When an out-of-town contractor comes into town they just slash his tyres! Their wages are high, and they get their work done by working together extremely well on site.

What they don't have is a middle ground. You can find firms in England that can produce a big

building by rationalised traditional methods. In America you either have to accept that everything is value-engineered – like brick slip stuck into polystyrene grooves – or over-arty and trendy. There's no middle ground for the ordinary professional American archtiect to survive in. He has a really hard time. Most places in America don't have our sort of town-planning system. If there's a cheaper way of building, the Contractor builds it. Here, if you don't please the local Planning Committee, it doesn't get built.

The 'signature architect' arose in America. I don't complain! Much of our work is overseas. But 'fame' can be sold by the yard, as mere wallpapering. Ironically, I had to go to Rice University, Houston, to be treated like a European architect; that is to say, as technically sophisticated, and to Holland to be treated like an American architect – as a wallpaper merchant! As a result, we had a brilliantly managed building production in America, and a badly-managed building production in the Netherlands.

**HC: Do you believe therefore that it's academia and the media that are creating the signature architects, rather than the public?**

JO: Yes, this is a sort of arts Mafia thing. It is very much part of New Labour.

When I did two projects for some developers, who had previously worked with Farrell and Grimshaw, they were invited to a working breakfast by Michael Heseltine. This was when he was Minister of the Environment in the Conservative government – it must have been 1981 or 1982 – and they refused to go. They thought if our bankers think we're turning into a kind of arty developers, they won't trust us – they won't trust us to build something really ugly and lucrative! That was what fame meant to the property people. It was bad news, ironically, in those days.

**HC: You said that when you went to Houston one of the first questions that the prospective client wanted to ask was whether you'd built any museums.**

JO: That's right. It was Gerald Heinz, the developer, who rang up to check me out. He called up SOM, and then SOM rang me and said, 'Heinz wants to know if you've built any museums. We thought you were building a university faculty in Houston.' I said, 'Yes, I am. What's this museum?' Then I understood. I wanted our calling cards to be over-printed with 'Museum-quality work guaranteed'.

Opposite left, top + bottom
Judge Institute of Management Studies, 1995.

Opposite right, top + bottom
Storm Water Pumping Station, Isle of Dogs, London, 1988.

Above
Glass structural columns for the Millennium Pavilion, an addition to Wadhurst Park, Sussex, 1999.

'Above all, John Outram, with his hectically-coloured and patterned, almost Romanesque buildings, with their fat, habitable, columns, offers a full blooded alternative to the Polite Moderns. His unique style is to be found (somewhat toned down) at the Judge Institute in Cambridge, and turned up to full volume at his new Duncan Hall at Rice University, Texas. Outram is, like the very different Miralles, uncategorisable. Which, after all the pigeonholing of a bluffer's guide, is rather refreshing.....and bodes well for an intriguing architectural future.'

Hugh Pearman, *Sunday Times*, 12 July 1998.

HC: And the flip side of lavishing all this architectural attention on museums and cultural buildings is that, you believe, the buildings that we're actually living and working in are totally neglected. Can you describe how the idea of the Existens Maximum – and how designing houses at Haverleij – wrestles with this particular chestnut?

JO: Well, what I've done is to turn functionalism completely on its head. Modern architecture, really, is the product of a collapse – the collapse of ornament, the collapse of form and the collapse of the whole Western architectural tradition. What was left was this notion of functionalism, practicality, material and all this stuff. These are all dregs really. They are theoretical dregs, *reductio ad* the lowest common factor. Out of it they tried to rebuild architecture. What I've done is to sort of decipher architecture. The net result is that what I call the frame now contains all the Vitruvian qualities. It contains the firmness, which is the machinery and the 'anti-gravity props' as I call them, rather than 'columns'.

HC: This whole idea of ornamenting and enriching our everyday living and working spaces runs counter to fame and celebrity and the attention which is given to Bilbao or the Pompidou Centre.

JO: When I went to Las Vegas on behalf of Battersea, I learnt that architects in Las Vegas only work as project managers now. They've been completely elbowed aside

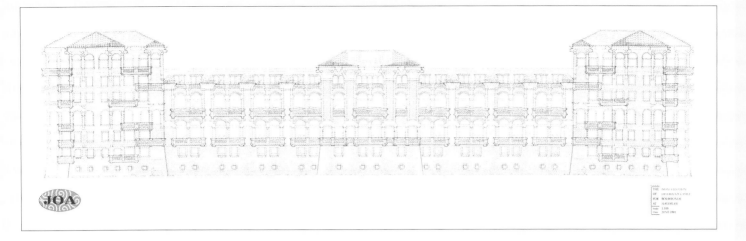

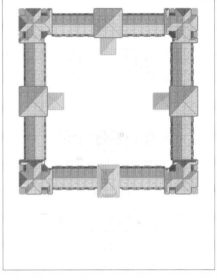

by illustrators and set designers. There's a vast territory of what you might call interior design that architecture has just lost control of because of this crisis, which was building up over the 19th century: the collapse of iconography and therefore decoration.

**HC: The quality and scope of your website is proof that your office is committed to engaging with a wider public. There's a directness about it – it's very much your words, your writing – which is rare. Most offices just put up project descriptions – something produced by the PR department. How important do you think disseminating ideas is, and how important do you think it is to have an authentic voice?**

JO: What I want to do is communicate to what I call ordinary literary people. I think if only that connection could be made, architects themselves would find a niche in our culture which they lack. They're presently having a hard time.

**HC: So you think that in a way celebrity and fame is a kind of distraction?**

JO: For me, yes. I also think the fact that the RIBA had to invite Tracy Emin to launch its Best Building of the Year in 2000 is the nadir. Architecture is the mother of the arts, not the orphan.

**HC: It suggests architecture is engaged with the novel and notoriety in the same way that, say, contemporary art is.**

JO: The Gallery Art industry has become the model for the architect. It produces odd-shaped buildings which aren't going to be much use to anybody. We have major problems constructing this strange artificial environment that human beings live in, and it just can't be constructed as a set of art objects.

**HC: In the long term, do you have faith that your vision is going to come through?**

JO: You mean in a large sense? Am I going to launch a movement or am I going to survive? I think I'm going to survive.

**HC: You seem just to have been true to yourself really.**

JO: Well, one thing has followed from another. I had to invent the walk-through column because we didn't win the competition for Bracken House because the bumps on the outside pushed the building inside, and that's bad news in the City. The walk-through column took the rentable territory right up to the property line. Then in Texas it turned out to be rather handy for rationalising the plan. Then I had to do something about concrete, because concrete is a lovely cheap material you can mould, but it looks ghastly when it gets old, so you colour it and pattern it. So there's always a practical side and a financial side, and then there's an intellectual side. They all sort of tumble over each other.

**HC: But it's certainly not an overt bid for longevity.**

JO: For celebrity or fame, you mean?

**HC: For fame over celebrity.**

JO: Well, I suppose you have to distinguish yourself, don't you? You have to be separate. Ultimately, you have to have a voice. ᴁ

Opposite
Anne and Charles Duncan Hall, Rice University, Houston, 1997.

Above
Elevation, section and roof plan for the Haverleij Castle project, 2001. John Outram's designs are part of a larger housing scheme master-planned by Sjoerd Soeters for Bouwfonds, 2001.

Notes
1. See John Outram, 'A Sixth Order', www.johnoutram.com.
2. Here Outram is quoting Bob Maxwell, who has said of Outram: 'He thinks for himself and dares to break the taboos (of Modernism)'.

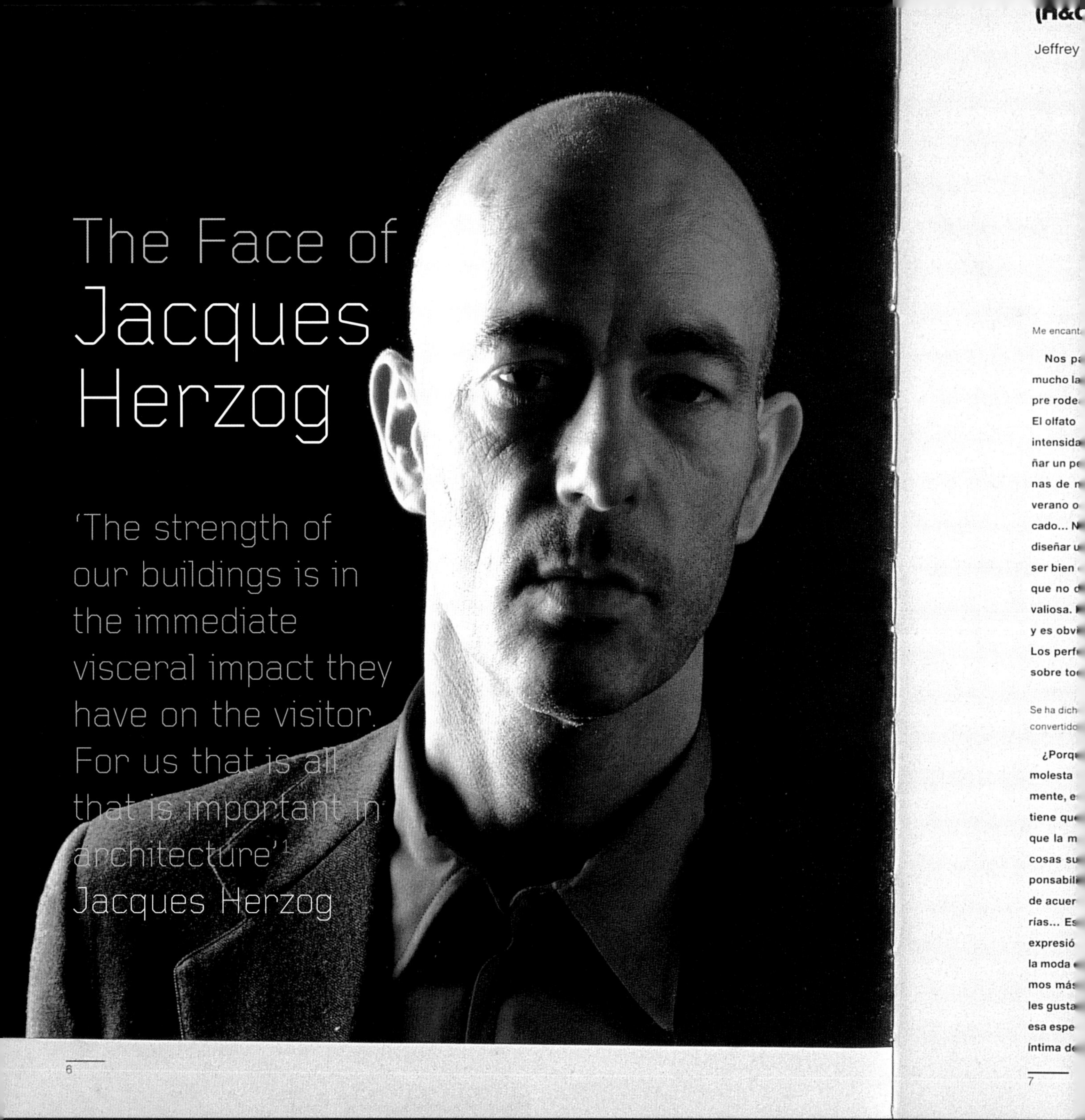

# The Face of Jacques Herzog

'The strength of our buildings is in the immediate visceral impact they have on the visitor. For us that is all that is important in architecture'[1]
Jacques Herzog

Me encant

Nos pa

mucho la

pre rode

El olfato

intensida

ñar un pe

nas de n

verano o

cado… N

diseñar u

ser bien

que no d

valiosa. 

y es obvi

Los perf

sobre to

Se ha dich

convertido

¿Porqu

molesta

mente, e

tiene qu

que la m

cosas su

ponsabili

de acuer

rías… Es

expresió

la moda 

mos más

les gusta

esa espe

íntima d

Julia Chance observes the phenomenon of the recurring and carefully-styled image of the face of Jacques Herzog as a new media phenomenon. She observes that, 'whereas we can recognise the faces of Richard Rogers, Norman Foster and Zaha Hadid from magazines, journals and television, Herzog and de Meuron stand out as architects who not only promote carefully composed seductive images of their buildings as desirable objects but also extend this vocabulary to include portraits of themselves – usually Jacques Herzog.' She shows how this notable shift is an advance on the more conventional means of media dissemination, which generally focus on photographs of built work or the words of architects.

### blueprint
ARCHITECTURE AND DESIGN

Extra:
the Tate
competition
in full

Toyo Ito
lightens up
Miyajima
in the dark

Mitterrand's
library

Furniture
loses weight

## The Swiss
bring art to
Bankside
*The Hitchcockian architecture of Herzog & de Meuron*

una conversación
con Jacques Herzog
(H&deM)

Jeffrey Kipnis

a conversation
with Jacques Herzog
(H&deM)

Jeffrey Kipnis

**45. CHAMPAGNE IN ECONOMY**
Leave it to regional carrier Crossair to serve Champagne. In this era of cutbacks, long may it last

**46. CLINIQUE LA MÉTAIRIE**
When everything goes wrong upstairs, this is one clinic worth having keyed in on your speed dial

**47. PETER ZUMTHOR**
Integrity, a respect for environment and a command of materials which is unmatched makes Mr. Zumthor one of the most important forces in architecture in the world and the gentleman we'd ask to design our ultimate mountain retreat

**48. BIRKHÄUSER BOOKS**
No one covers the world of architecture as thoroughly as this Basel-based publisher

**49. SIMMENTAL**
Another happy cow that is well mannered and on a handsome royalty deal with Lindt

SWISS TOP 50

Above: clockwise from top left
Jacques Herzog as featured on the cover of the March 1995 issue of *Blueprint*; Jacques Herzog on the inside pages of *el croquis*'s monograph *Herzog & de Meuron 1993-1997*, no 84, 1997; Jacques Herzog featured in the 'Swiss Top 50' in *Wallpaper*, May 2001.

Opposite
Detail from Jacques Herzog on the inside pages of *el croquis*'s monograph *Herzog & de Meuron 1993-1997*, no 84, 1997

Herzog and de Meuron have created a number of varied and daring architectural works often of exceptional quality. The sophistication of their practice lies not only in the creation of remarkable buildings but also in their understanding of how to work productively with, rather than naively alongside, the methods and the forms with which the contemporary media represents architecture and architects. This essay investigates the way in which we are presented with the image of the face of Jacques Herzog over time, and how this contributes to a more general understanding of the presence and activities of the practice.

During the 1996 Channel Four series which recorded the progress of the the Bankside Power Station transformation into the Tate Modern Gallery, Jacques Herzog was seen instructing a member of the camera crew not to film him from the angle that the cameraman had adopted because, Herzog claimed, he did not look good from that angle.

This incident could, I propose, be understood as more than a one-off event in which Jacques Herzog let his narcissism get the better of him.

While Herzog and de Meuron claim that the practice's architecture, 'is understood only by means of itself, with no aids to understanding', his instructions to the BBC cameraman described above is an example of a level of attention paid by the practice to a more far-reaching construction of meaning around their architectural projects than that derived from subjective experience of the buildings alone.

The way in which Herzog and de Meuron's projects are understood is not, as Herzog suggests, exclusively in the encounter between subject and building, in the 'immediate visceral impact that they have on the visitor' - however impressive this may be - but is also substantially informed by the impact that the media networks have on our perception of the projects and the architects themselves.

The example of Jacques Herzog's behaviour recounted above, describes a typical level of control that Herzog and de Meuron exert over media representations not only of their architectural projects but also of themselves. In the last few years they have authorised extensive publications and television coverage about their building projects and about the practice, not only in books solely dedicated to their works but also in a wide range of lifestyle magazines with world-wide distribution.

One of the many ways in which the practice's renown has been established will be addressed here and that is the phenomenon in the last years of the recurring appearance of the image of the face of Jacques Herzog throughout the information networks. Carefully composed, moody portraits have for some time been frequenting the pages of style-conscious magazines such as *Blueprint* and *Wallpaper* and whereas we can recognise the faces of Richard Rogers, Norman Foster and Zaha Hadid from magazines, journals and television, Herzog and de Meuron stand out as architects who not only promote carefully composed seductive images of their buildings as desirable objects but also extend this vocabulary to include portraits of themselves - usually Jacques Herzog.

In any one publication, the face of Jacques Herzog is often as large if not larger than the images of the buildings which are described and with this intense focus on the face of the architect, carefully modelled in light and with a similar expression despite a lapse in years between publications the cultural myth underlying the

acknowledgement of the architectural presence of Herzog and de Meuron, has been elaborated.

The building projects of Herzog and de Meuron vary considerably in appearance and are renowned for the way in which their external surfaces are treated. Extensive design time and energy is spent working on the often highly inventive building envelopes created to enclose the spaces within, the qualities of the latter often being comparatively unspectacular.[3]

A new palette of signifiers is chosen for each project, for each new circumstance. The surface qualities of the envelope often contain references to things beyond the buildings themselves, for example the external window grilles of the luxury Apartments in Schützenmattstrasse, Basel which were developed from the observations of cast iron street drainage gutters, or the way in which the external wall panels on the storage building for the Ricola factory in Laufen refer to the familiar sight of a shelving system.[4]

This visual diversity of the projects means that for the untrained eye and for the time before their widespread renown, a building designed by Herzog and de Meuron would not easily have been identified as

'It stands there, as if it created itself, without the laughable particularity of the author, without his mark.... The architecture is understood only by means of itself, with no aids to understanding, capable of being produced only out of architecture, not out of anecdotes or quotes or functional processes. Architecture is its own substantiality in it's location.'[2] *Jacques Herzog and Pierre de Meuron*

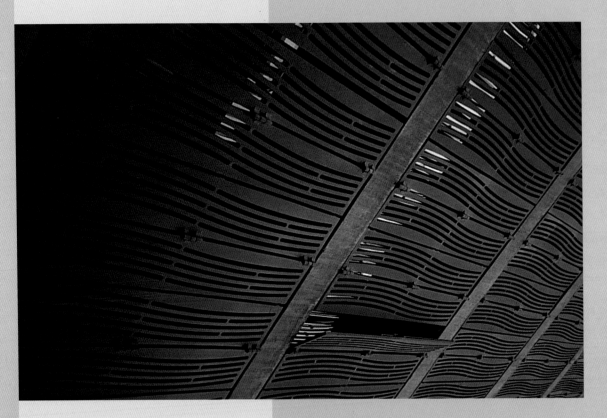

being designed by them. There is no easily recognisable house style in their projects, and it takes some time to detect a house sensibility. Given the often reported over-load of information that we are generally subjected to and the resultant tendency to forget very quickly images and names of the moment as more information arrives on the scene, there would always have been a possibility that Herzog and de Meuron's series of diverse projects could be perceived as a series of fragments without acknowledgement of the consistency of their authorship.

Although there is no easily recognisable style of the buildings of Herzog and de Meuron, over the years and through a diversity of publications the recurrence of the image of the sculpted face with shaven hair, the trace of stubble and the gradual, sensual signs of ageing present the same photogenic qualities that James Russell identified as being present in the building projects, 'muscular massing and textural richness'.[5]

The expression on the face of Jacques Herzog will never be altered by frivolous changes of mood and this indicates desirable qualities of both building and architect; perseverance, stamina and consistency. Although ageing may eventually gently modify the image, the expression, the stare and the poise will remain steady. The face of Jacques Herzog appears in different publications over the years as a visual constant behind the diversity of history, place,

circumstance, project and fashion. It is a face that promises to be capable of remaining static amid the fleetingness of contemporary life and the ravages of architectural practice.

In style and quality the portrait bears similarities to images that we are used to seeing of rock and pop stars. However, whereas for these stars the body and the face are more implicitly linked to the immediate product being presented – the song is sung and the dance is danced – the relevance of the architect's face presented in relation to the product offered is not so immediately obvious. But the relevance can be understood with reference to the careful construction of the general perception of Herzog and de Meuron.

To add to the effect of the practice's name being mentioned in the architectural news, the recurring appearance of the face of Jacques Herzog throughout the media networks has ensured that a consistent and memorable image has been connected to the diversity of projects produced. But the face of Jacques Herzog is not just the face of an architect behind the work and the practice as we are used to seeing in magazines, at opening ceremonies or reclining on a chair in a television interview discussing a project from a distance. The consistently presented and carefully composed image of the face of Jacques Herzog is as inherent in the construction of the myth of the practice of Herzog and de Meuron as are the buildings and the images of the buildings themselves. As the painfully slow (compared to other fields of production) process of building demands a level of patience from the audience between each presentation on the scene of newly completed goods, the steady, intermittent distribution of the face with its surfaces as carefully modelled in light by the photographer as are those of the building envelopes by the architect, our insatiable desire for the striking and highly styled image has been satisfied and the architect who was busy and out of sight not forgotten.

Thus, with the regular distribution of the portrait and the level of control exerted over it's representation (as demonstrated by Jacques Herzog's instructions to the cameraman in the Channel Four documentary) the charismatic presence of the practice is sustained.

Whereas Madonna's image is renewed to satisfy the requirements and cycles of fashion of the pop market, the haunting consistency of the portrait of Jacques Herzog over time respects the principle that the qualities underlying decent architecture should last longer than the cycles of fashion, implying reassuringly that in architecture there may still be some eternal truths.

Although Herzog is only half of the name of the practice, Herzog and de Meuron and a fraction of the present team, the image distributed at regular intervals could only be of one face. Two faces would be harder to record at different times with the same consistent qualities and two faces would be compared with one another causing distraction.

Architecture is a field in which a game is played as practices compete to be in the position of what Pierre Bourdieu calls, the 'consecrated avant garde';[6] those whose work has architectural qualities that are acknowledged as being worthy and possessing symbolic capital that has been valorised by people in positions of influence. Such a position is distinguished from the majority of architects who find themselves as their careers develop operating as run of the mill building designers achieving comparatively little cultural status for their efforts. Compared to the enormous number of practising architects, the number of places for the 'consecrated avant garde' is limited. Contemporary architectural practices are aware of this and of the benefits of establishing a position for themselves in the field; a dramatic increase in potential for jobs due to media coverage and ultimately as renown ensues, an increased autonomy in the way that they will be able to make buildings and landscapes. Increasingly sophisticated means are being used to compete by the generations that have grown up observing the mechanics of the media.

In his book, *The Favored Circle*, Garry Stevens writes,

'would-be avant gardes seek labels to distinguish their products from others. To a

Notes
1. Jacques Herzog, 'A conversation with Jacques Herzog [H&de M]', *Jeffrey Kipnis*, Herzog and de Meuron 1983–1993, *el croquis* (Madrid), 1993, p 18.
2. Jacques Herzog and Pierre de Meuron, 'Passionate Infidelity' in *Mack, Herzog & de Meuron 1989–1991*, Gerard Mack, ed. Birkhäuser (Basle), p 182.
3. Tate Modern stands out as an exception here.
4. These references are enjoyable for their simplicity and playfulness. They also mean that the buildings are photogenic, potentially triggering relationships with neighbouring images in the context of the magazine.
5. James Russell, 'Fading Photographs', Harvard Design Magazine, Fall (1998) p 44. Also in 'Sculptural Values, the Use and Application of Sculptural Qualities in the Works of Herzog and de Meuron', MSc report by Sarah Jackson for The Bartlett School of Architecture, University College London, September 1999.
6. Garry Stevens, *The Favored Circle: The Social Foundations of Architectural Distinction*, The MIT Press (Cambridge, MA, and London) 1998, p 100.
7. Ibid, p 99.
8. Jean Baudrillard, The Evil Demon of Images, Power Institute Publications (Sydney), 1987, p 13.

In a culture with a short term memory and a habit of consuming large quantities of highly sophisticated visual images the recurrence of a practice´s name is no longer enough to establish or sustain a level of renown.

great extent these labels do not so much as serve to mark a new avant garde position as to create it, to produce the very difference it attempts to express. The right to name is a crucial part of the struggles between avant gardes.'[7]

In a culture with a short-term memory and a habit of consuming large quantities of highly sophisticated visual images, the recurrence of a practice´s name is no longer enough to establish or sustain a level of renown. The recurring portrait of Jacques Herzog can be understood as being a kind of label, a constant visual reference point for the diversity of projects recurring through the information networks over time. A subtle kind of label which, in its making and delivery is tuned to the contemporary consciousness. Over time, the recurring image of the portrait combined with that of the sight and sound of the practice's name links up in the mind with the images, and possibly experiences, of the diversity of building projects and thus the phenomenon of Herzog and de Meuron is established and strengthened.

Because we know about and eagerly await the next well-publicised project, the phenomenon of Herzog and de Meuron is so well established that it will be difficult if not impossible for any of their buildings to, 'stand(s) there, as if it created itself'. The indication of authorship of the projects is much more subtle and more suited to our media-luxuriant culture than there simply being recognisable visual qualities within the buildings themselves.

Being as famous as Herzog and de Meuron means that we the public know so many details about each project before it has left their office that there is no opportunity for it to 'stand(s) there, as if it created itself'; publicity has preempted experience, 'images' as Baudrillard said some years ago, 'precede the real'.[8]

However, the steady stare of Jacques Herzog will continue to be delivered through the networks reassuring us that there is a consistency, and a stability in this practice, as well as a lot of style. ∆

Julia Chance is an architect, teacher and free lance writer.

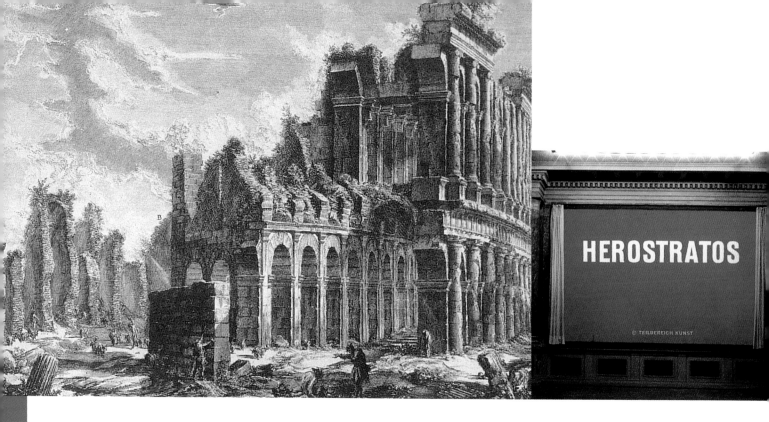

# Fame + Ruins

Following on from the premise that fame and ruins are inextricably linked, Heinz Schütz looks at the examples of Herostratos, who was sentenced to death for the destruction of the temple of Artemis in 356 BC and the demolition of parts of the housing estate Pruitt Igoe in St Louis, USA, in 1972. Likening Herostratos to the idea of modernism in that he was willing to break the rules and thus risk his own existence, Schütz also observes ruins to be a central topos of postmodernism.

### Herostratus

In 1980 a group of artists called Teilbereich Kunst (art department)[1] published the name of a man whom judges sentenced to death more than 2,000 years ago so that he would not enter the collective memory – or at least that is what they intended. In the streets of Munich the group billposted the encyclopaedic explanation:

'man who set fire to a temple in order to be immortal.'

A wall painting in the hall of the Munich arts academy spelt out – in white capital letters on a red background – the name of the desecrator of the temple: HEROSTRATOS. By destroying the temple of Artemis at Ephesos – a shrine that was one of the seven wonders of the ancient world – in his yearning for fame, Herostratos was pursuing his aim to enter history. In order to undermine this aim, the legend goes, the court when it sentenced him in 356 BC also made mentioning his name punishable by death. The judges' threat failed. The ancient historian

Theopompus had already named the desecrator.[2] Today Herostratos is listed in encyclopaedias.

The publishing of the name Herostratos as part of an art event occurred at a time when the happily progressive programme of modernism and its quest for permanent innovation was increasingly being overtaken by events. At the beginning of the 1980s the debate about Post-Modernism slowly started to heat up. It reached a climax during that decade, only to cool down noticeably by the millennium and can be understood as a symptom of the crisis that modernity found itself in, regardless of whether one sees Post-Modernism as the death of modernism or as its critically analytical continuation. The trend in the theoretical and aesthetic discourse of Post-Modernism is directed towards the topos of memory.

Here the model of history as a permanent progression becomes obsolete. Although, of course, it must not be forgotten that the simple linear model of progress has already been questioned by modernists and enlightened social philosophers – for example, in Walter Benjamin's theory of the ruins of history,

Adorno's and Horkheimer's dialectic of enlightenment and Ernst Bloch's reflections on simultaneity and the nonsimultaneous.

While memory becomes a central point of reference in Post-Modern thinking and aesthetics, simple progressive thinking survives unharmed and is at the same time naturalised in the field of technology – one invention follows hard on another – and in the market economy which is based on an ideology of permanent growth.

Herostratos, the name published in the hall of the arts academy, touches upon the Post-Modern topos of memory and the condition of avant-gardism. Herostratos' crime can, at least partially, be seen as being on a par with the ideals of modernism: he broke the existing rules, he broke through to taboos and as he did so he risked his own existence. One avant-gardist aim is to bridge the gulf between art and life. In complete contrast to the emergence of modern art, which was directed against places of eternal truth and ever-valid rules in a rather anti-academic fashion, and against places of authority and representation, the avant-garde became academic towards the end of the 20th century. And although the avant-gardists, particularly the Futurists, fought the museum as a passive cult place as early as at the start of the 20th century, and the artists of the second avant-garde wave in the 1960s negated traditional institutions in order to advance to the everyday, they were caught up by the museum. Artists now rely on museums in order to continue to be recognised.

Modernism has entered a state of self-acquisition and self-referencing – most obviously in appropriation art and eclectic neo-Neoclassicism in architecture. It repeats itself as a quotation. The utopian impetus has made way for the impetus of memory. The radicalism of Herostratos can be compared to the ideals of a radical modernism. But while the avant-gardistes break existing rules in order to potentially change history, Herostratos committed a crime only in order to enter it. He desecrated the temple and thereby indirectly killed himself. The ruin, as will be explained below, is a sign of Post-Modernism.[3] Herostratos' crime was aimed at his fame in posterity. The receptive other side of this fame after death is memory, a central topos of Post-Modernism. And, in this context, the question about the meaning of fame arises.

Teilbereich Kunst saw in the search for fame a model of the current production of culture, which is determined by the laws of the market:

The will to communication becomes compulsive through a culture determined by the exchange of goods, to be realised through the media, i.e. to make up for the subjective powerlessness with the power of the immortalising medium. Herostratos, the counterexample to the classical Greek human ideal, is thus not an expression of the turning point of the contemporary production of art, but is indeed the equivalent of the nature of this art production.[4]

And, indeed, as part of the market art production is dependent on being present in the media. In market terms the reputation of a product or a name raises its value. In order to be noticed the cultural producer is obliged to express himself or herself through the media. A presence in the media is a prerequisite for the survival in technocapitalism. However, the compulsion to this presence is followed by a simultaneous double existence: on the one hand there are the real producers and the real products, the people and the objects; on the other, there are the images, logos and labels. The omnipresence of the media contributes to fame not only in the sense of a quantitative expansion but, turning around Walter Benjamin's sentence that reproduction causes the desubstantiation of the original, the reproductive medium today markets the substantiation of the original. Independent of the quality of a product, independent of the performance of a person, the media can manage, at least for some time, to award it or them a substance, an aura *sui generis*. Andy Warhol's promise to make everybody into a star for a few minutes by pointing the camera at them hints at this direction.

In that the often short-lived 'fame' produced by the media dominates in technocapitalism, it is distinguished from the fame after death for which Herostratos paid with his life. The will to the latter is by no means forced by the laws of an 'exchange of goods', but this kind of fame obviously acts as an end in itself, to which all other ends are subordinate. Following his will to fame after death, an irreconcilable paradox unfolded in Herostratos' person. Knowing that his action would be punished by death – and that only when he was known as the culprit would his crime make any sense at all – he set fire to the temple. He sacrificed his life in order to be famous after his death – so that his name would circulate in posterity. Even if his sacrifice had been successful – and that was by no means guaranteed – he would not have been able to perceive its success when he was dead. With his death the idea of posterity, which only existed for him as a phantasm when he was alive, vanished for him. Adapting Duchamp's statement – 'In fact it is always only the others who die' – one can equally say about fame after death: 'In fact there is only such thing as fame after death of others.' The will to fame after death follows an analogy which seemingly refers to the self but which, in the end, applies only to the others. As in any example of fame during life, the resonance that the I triggers off in the You – even if it is only by the calling of a name – seems to cause an empowering potentiating of the I.

The Herostratos paradox comes into being when a nominal trap snaps shut. A euphemism that is often used talks of 'immortality' instead of 'fame after death'. The word suggests that if a name circulates, possibly for centuries, the holder of that name has become 'immortal'. Religions usually encourage a belief in life after death. In the case of Herostratos there are no indications to allege religiousness. On the contrary, the violation of the temple and the sin thus committed imply a religious distance. He tried to win the immortality assigned to the goddess by a sin directed against the goddess herself. Thus he fell into the nominal trap: he put the potential survival of his name above his own survival – the gods are regarded as immortal, although only their names are known. Absurdly, the potential mention of his name and ensuring his place in posterity were worth more to him than his life.

### Pruitt-Igoe

On 15 July 1972 the central residential tower blocks of Pruitt-Igoe in St Louis, Missouri, were blown up. The settlement was designed by Minoru Yamasaki, the World Trade Center architect, and his design in the International Style won an award from the American Institute of Architects. The housing was built in the middle of the1950s. However, living conditions there proved increasingly desolate:

During the 1970s the blasting of Pruitt-Igoe attained its symbolic transubstantiation: its demolition was declared to be the end of modernism and the beginning of Post-Modernism. The invention and spreading of this myth is due to Charles Jencks, who said about his lectures in the year 1974:

> The idea of a sudden end, in conjunction with slides of the explosion, had an enormously liberating effect. During the following two years I used this rhetorical formula in lectures around the world – death of modernity/beginning of Post-Modernity, knowing that it was a symbolic invention (I even made up a false date), and was still pleasantly surprised to see that almost everybody, especially the press, accepted it as the truth.[6]

Although Jencks emphasises that his 'arguments are symbolic, or ironic caricatures', this does not stop the images of the demolition being understood, at least partially, as a

liberation from modernism which was clearly seen as a burden. In architecture this discomfort with modernism, which was marked by the primacy of economic factors, may have been due to an amalgamation of architectonic-aesthetic ideologies with problematic social structures. Yet the myth of the origin of Post-Modernism elevates itself above the factual – 'I even made up a false date'. Like any myth, it does not ultimately need a historical anchoring; in place of the real it has its own logic.

The origin myth, with the help of which Post-Modernism became stylised into an epoch, gains substance in the context of the picture of the imploding architecture. This image, which the thereby constructed Post-Modernism carries as a banner and in which it is mirrored, is that of a ruin. Yet the word 'ruin', when it refers to the picture of Pruitt-Igoe, does not refer to rocks and remains of walls but to architecture at the moment of destruction. Under the law of acceleration that prevails in technocapitalism, the ruin exists only in the moment of its collapse. Under the law of image-making that prevails in today's media society, the ruin exists only as an image. As the building disappears it becomes a dynamic imposing ruin for a few moments: it freezes to a photographic sequence. The implosion thus frozen into the image becomes a topos in the debate between modernists and Post-Modernists. Taking up the aggressiveness of the myth of the origin of Post-Modernism, Tony Vidler polemicises against Jencks with images which, according to Jencks – happy, as it were, that his invention has worked – 'showed my skull as it breaks into pieces in slow motion like Pruitt-Igoe'.[7]

Jencks puts the image of the imploding architecture, of the ruin to be exact, at the beginning of Post-Modernism. This image of the blasting has the capability to recall memories of the futuristic glorification of explosive power, or the continuously aggressive innovationism of the former avant-garde. It could be interpreted as a triumph of the hopeful new over the old, in which case the point would be that the old – modernism – had itself always been reliant on the new. Looking at it in this way, what would be the new beyond the new? The image of the demolition does not answer this question; it does not show the other. But the fascination of the image is the image itself: the imploding architecture, the ruin at the moment of its creation.

What, in general, is the potential fascination of ruins?

### 'Oh les belles, les sublimes ruines!'

Ruins are always a sign of defeat. What has been built up in hope breaks down. It breaks down slowly over time or quickly in case of a catastrophe, or it is destroyed on purpose. In the best case this purposeful destruction is to make room for other buildings but often, as, for example, in war, it is for strategic reasons born out of hatred and revenge. The aim is only to cause damage. In that sense, a moment of failure, or even desperation, is inscribed in ruins. Nevertheless, throughout the course of history a differently evolved fascination with ruins has unfolded itself, which is closely connected to concepts like transitoriness, solemnity and fame.

In the context of a romantically founded understanding of ruins, for example, Georg Simmel emphasised the relation of ruins to nature. To him, ruins are renaturalised artefacts in which nature, so to speak, takes back what has been taken from it.

Far from the romantic understanding of nature, the Post-Modern architectural discourse is more closely linked to the solemnity that Denis Diderot saw in ruins. The ruin-portraits by Hubert Robert created in him a feeling of 'sweet melancholy'. Beyond the sentimental, he calls the ruins 'beautiful' and 'solemn'. 'Ruins let me have solemn ideas. Everything is destroyed, everything breaks away, everything passes away. Only the world remains. Only time carries on. How old is our world! I wander between two eternities.'

As Hubert Burda has demonstrated, there is a close link between Diderot's understanding of ruins and Burke's reflections on their solemnity. Diderot particularly repeats Burke's descriptive terms – vastness, infinity and magnitude. From the viewpoint of the solemn, the sight of a ruin causes the diminution of the person looking at it. It evokes a grandeur that overwhelms the onlooker in one way, but in which he or she also takes part in another way. In the simultaneity of overwhelming and elevation, the imagination of the solemn transcends history.

The discovery of a historical dimension in the wreckage of ruins has played a decisive role in their treatment since the Renaissance. Only after the humanistic interest in antiquity had been awakened and ancient Rome had been glorified did the ruins of the past, still serving as quarries until the 16th century, find recognition. Archaeological awareness was directed at them; the fantasy of, for instance, Giovanni Battista Piranesi was sparked off by them. The re-evaluation of the ruin from a quarry to the relic of a highly regarded antiquity immediately made itself evident in artificial ruins which were copied from antique models and built in gardens, and in the transition of broken antique sculptures into an autonomous genre: the torso. In the context of an idealised past, the negative of

destruction flowed positively into the artificial ruin and the torso. The ideal that lay in ruins was transferred to the ruins.

With the re-evaluation of Roman ruins, which were read as symbolising the former glory of Rome, a model of ruins as fame after death was evolving. It reached even into the 20th century and was picked up by Hitler's architect Albert Speer. In order to further increase Hitler's fame after death, Speer developed a 'theory of the value of ruins':

Buildings constructed in a modern way, what was their starting point, were clearly little suited to create that 'bridge of traditions' to future generations demanded by Hitler: unthinkable that a rusting heap of ruins would communicate the heroic inspiration that Hitler adored in the monuments of the past. My 'theory' was meant to counteract this dilemma. The use of special materials as well as taking into account special constructional considerations was meant to enable the buildings, in a state of dilapidation after hundreds, or (so we reckoned) thousands of years, to appear similar to the Roman models.

The hypertrophied will to fame after death, which during Hitler's dictatorship resulted not only in monumental architecture but also in a world war, the Holocaust and overwhelming destruction, anticipates the ruin as an ideal carrier of fame. It suggests itself to apply Saul Friedländer's analyses in 'Kitsch and death' to Speer's theoretically anticipated ruins.

Returning to the demolition of Pruitt-Igoe, in the architectural discourse the image of the implosion acted as an aggressive 'argument', which launched a theory and which thus, in the end, can also be seen as part of the attempt to build up the fame of the theoretician. The image of the blasting, which generates the victory of Post-Modernism over modernism in this discourse, touches upon the image of ruins as a central topos of Post-Modernism: the overcoming of history as a ruin of history, in a hall of fame in which time has come to a standstill. At the close of the 20th century there was – and there still is – the real threat of an ecological collapse, an arms build-up and forced economies. On a symbolic level a type of apocalyptic bliss has developed, a yearning for solemnity and for exiting from history. In a compensatory manner, both levels find their symbolically transfigured expression in the image of the frozen implosion.

Translated: Anne Dieterich (June 2001)

*Heinz Schütz studied theatre, history of art, philosophy and German in Munich and Vienna, and obtained a PhD in 1984. Since 1985 he has worked as a freelance writer and art critic. He is a regular contributor to* Kunstforum international *and teaches at LMU and the Akademie der Bildenden Künste in Munich.*

**Notes**
1. 'Herostratos' was the only action of Teilbereich Kunst, which broke up soon after the event. Its members were Rudolf Herz, Stephan Huber and Thomas Lehnerer.
2. Peter Moritz Pickshaus: *Destroyers of Art – Case Studies: Motives and Psychogrammes*, (Reinbek), 1988, pp 36–8.
3. See also Hannes Böhringer, 'The Ruins of Posthistory' in *Hannes Böhringer, Begriffsfelder. Von der Philosophie zur Kunst*, (Berlin), 1993, p 37.
4. Teilbereich Kunst, Herostratos, 1980 in Rudolf Herz and Thomas Lehnerer, *Rot ist dann nur noch die Farbe des Blutes*, (Baden-Baden), 1993, p 37.
5. Tom Wolfe, *From Bauhaus To Our House*, Eng.
6. Charles Jencks, *Die Postmoderne. Der neue Klassizismus in Kunst und Architektur*, Eng.
7. Ibid.

# Word of Mouth

Diller + Scofidio
in conversation
with Jayne Merkel

Despite today's continual barrage of printed publications and numbing blitz of electronic images, the fastest rising stars in New York, Ricardo Scofidio and Elizabeth Diller, maintain that they still find out about most things by WORD OF MOUTH. The partners talk to Jayne Merkel, editor of *Oculus* magazine, about their relatively new found architectural eminence. (Celebrated by the art world and academic community since the founding of their office in 1979, they have practiced at the edge of the architectural radar producing few built works until now.) The first architects to receive a McArthur Foundation 'genius grant' in 1999, a major retrospective of their work is also planned for 2003 at the Whitney Museum in New York.

Ricardo Scofidio and Elisabeth Diller

Slither Housing, Kitagata Housing, Gifu, Japan, completed 2000. A low-cost housing block that is part of a larger complex master-planned by Arata Isozaki, the Slither Building resists the standardisation that occurs in most social housing schemes. The apartment block takes a reptilian, slightly curving, form that allows each apartment to stand alone. Organised into fifteen vertical stacks of seven units, each of the vertical stacks are at a slight angle to each other. The plan of each apartment is also designed to slip by 1.4 m so that no home exactly mirrors its neighbour. Each floor slab is offset vertically by a gap of 200 mm.

Top
The elevation of the Slither Building defines a courtyard that further defies uniformity by creating space for public art.

Middle left
Night view of the outside corridor. The single loaded corridor is staggered allowing each resident direct entry through their individual front door. The ramp of the corridor is tilted to accommodate the 200-mm gap between each floor slab.

Middle right
Side view from the ground of the courtyard side of the building, revealing the angles of the perforated metal screen cladding.

**Diller+Scofidio**, who are married, practise together in a low-voltage, nuts and bolts loft upstairs from *Village Voice* offices on Cooper Square, across the street from the Cooper Union, where Scofidio has taught since 1967. Diller, who was once his student, has been teaching at Princeton University since 1990. Last year they completed the Slither Building, a serpentine low-income housing project in Gifu, Japan. At about the same time the Brasserie Restaurant opened in the Seagram Building in New York. Suddenly everything is changing. Later this year their Blur Building, an exposition pavilion engulfed in mist on Lake Neuchatel, at Yverdon-les-Bains in Switzerland, will be ready for visitors. This interview took place in the summer of 2001, only weeks after the pair had been selected to design their first museum, the Institute of Contemporary Art (ICA) in Boston.

Jayne Merkel: You've always been, by your own admission, 'provocateurs.' Can you still be out on the edge when you're certified geniuses?
Elisabeth Diller: All the more when you've been certified. You have more energy for provocations. After 20 years, the MacArthur Foundation finally decided to recognise architecture and chose our anomalous practice for the first award. It's a perfect validation. The architectural discipline can no longer dismiss us as fringe – they have to contend with us.
Ricardo Scofidio: When we began working together we never intended to build up an office that graduated from small to big projects. We were in it for the pleasure. We still are. After the Brasserie, a deluge of calls came in from prospective restaurateurs. But the thought of doing another restaurant was not very appealing. I guess we have the Stanley Kubrick syndrome, we want to experiment with every genre once. We don't want to keep doing the same movie over and over.

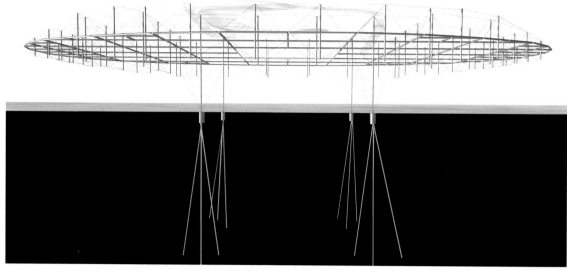

**Blur Building, Expo 2002, Yverdon-les-Bains, Switzerland**, due for completion beginning of 2002. The structure of this media centre, located at the base of Lake Neuchatel, will not be entirely visible from the shore. The 300-foot-wide and 200-foot-deep artificial cloud surrounding the pavilion is formed out of filtered lake water shot a fine mist through 34,000 nozzles. Prior to entering the Blur Building via a ramped bridge, each visitor responds to a questionnaire/character profile and receives a 'braincoat' (smart raincoat). Protective clothing, these raincoats also encourage visitors' interaction. As people pass one another, their coats will compare profiles and change colour – an electronic blush - indicating a degree of attraction or repulsion.

Above top
Tensegrity view of
Blur Building.

Middle left
Full view of the building.

Middle centre
Braincoat station.

Middle Right
The Angel Bar at the
summit of the building.

Right
Perspective of Bar

Bottom
The 'braincoat' that visitors
are given to wear on entering
the building.

ED: The McArthur Foundation is known for backing independents who don't play by the rules so that they can continue to not play by the rules. The validation could never tame us. It did, however, have a practical effect. It allowed us to free up some time from income-producing endeavours to lubricate the way for new work. Both of us are taking alternate semesters off from teaching for the five-year term of the fellowship. Our work continues to be research oriented, whether intended for print, art installation or even a public building. It doesn't matter if it's tiny or big, our approach guarantees that it will always be unprofitable.
RS: The work follows certain lines of research, though the medium changes continuously. Whether it's architecture, performance or artefact the work is guided by an outside agenda. After the MacArthur and the Brasserie, a larger scale of work started to come our way, with bigger budgets. Since the ICA, all eyes seem to be upon us. It may be difficult to keep the multiple disciplines in play for the next few years. We will have to focus.
**JM: I noticed that you dropped out of the [New York] Sculpture Center competition. It's really rare to turn things down.**
ED: We also just turned down a great opportunity to work with Enrique Norten on a new fine arts college in Mexico City. For us, to get into a project in depth means to accept its all-consuming nature. That means we have to radically edit our endeavours to engage the chaotic methodology of a big project. There's never a logical solution at the end of a linear process. You work hard, throw out 98 per cent

of the experiments and salvage the remaining two per cent. It looks facile from the outside.

JM: Are there downsides as you become more and more visible?

RS: Before people paid attention, we were happy outsiders. Now there's pressure to stay dissident.

JM: Frank Gehry said the same thing after the Guggenheim Bilbao opened.

RS: Visibility inflates prices. When we originally designed the Slow House [1991] the estimated construction cost was reasonable. After it received a PA award and the models were bought by MOMA for their permanent collection, construction costs shot up.

JM: There was even somebody who stole it. I don't know if you know that. There was a competition at the Contemporary Arts Center in Cincinnati for a house show, and the winning project sounded exactly like the Slow House. That happens.

ED: Work gets disseminated quickly into print media and instantly absorbed into architectural culture. That means you have to move fast.

JM: It's not even absorbed, just taken in at a glance. With television and the Internet information is processed almost instantaneously, but architecture takes time to conceive and design, and build.

RS: It's a slow art.

ED: The trap is, of course, that people that are hot today cool off tomorrow. We don't think too much about it. We've been working at our own pace, doing one project after another for

20 years, and we're going to continue whether there's a market for it or not. If the work is compelling to us, it will probably be interesting to others.

There's another issue about time. Many of our projects were ephemeral installations. We conceived a project, realised it very quickly in public space, elicited a response and then dumped it in landfill. Now all of the sudden we are working on buildings that are here to stay. The ICA will be a new museum of contemporary art. The architecture of the museum for contemporary art must for ever be contemporary; it must live in the perpetual present. What is the language of permanent newness? Wright somehow managed it in the Guggenheim.

JM: It is interesting that that works. I don't think there is completely a test of time, because certain things do go in and out of favour, but certain things remain. The Laurentian Library is still interesting, and the Guggenheim is still a kind of surprise.

ED: It's not repeatable, it's a one-off.

RS: Because it has to do with space.

JM: To what extent does fame, celebrity, prominence, reputation make you aware of people? Who, what do you look at?

ED: You wouldn't believe the trash we look at. Gossip, fashion and conspiracy theory magazines. Ric subscribes to *Aviation Weekly* and doesn't fly a plane. At the same time, we read critical theory and academic journals. We like to mix it up between popular and academic culture. We tend to pass over the [architecture] magazines.

RS: We tend to travel outside of the architectural crowd and fraternise more with directors, curators, new media people, writers. There's always a crosscurrent of activity. We tend to get dragged by our non-architect friends to see and/or read things in unexpected places.

JM: You mean despite all the media, what you actually look at is suggested by word of mouth?

ED: Yes, Word of mouth still works.

JM: What magazines have you been in?

This page
**The Brasserie, Seagram Building, New York City, 2000.** The Seagram Building is perhaps the single most iconic building of the 20th century. Designed by Mies van der Rohe in 1954, it contained two renowned Manhattan eateries – the Four Seasons Restaurant and the Brasserie - designed by Philip Johnson. When the Brasserie was destroyed by fire in 1995, Seagram heiress Phyllis Lambert persuaded the restaurant's owners to hire Diller + Scofidio to redesign the space. Located in the base of the glass tower, the architects made a conscious decision to make the restaurant, which has no views out, all about looking and being seen, emphasizing through the dramatic entrance stair and through the presence of cameras and TV screens the social and theatrical aspects of dining. The rough original concrete surfaces of Johnson's interior space were relined with new skins of wood, terrazzo, tile and glass. Its most prominent feature is the pearwood ceiling that peels down, moulding into seating as to create a continuous wrapper around the dining space.

Above top left
The Brasserie's pearwood curved wrapper.

Above bottom left
Private booths, partitioned by tall upholstered slabs, flank the dining area.

Above top right
Dining Room in Diller + Scofidio's Brasserie in the Seagram Building.

Above bottom right
Girl at the bar in the Brasserie. Above the bar are TV screens that show the image of the last 15 people to enter the restaurant.

ED: We had a nice feature in *Wired* last year. A stream of architecture magazines. I think the biggest testament to our accomplishment would be if we got featured in *People*. I could tell my mother to look for us on her supermarket tabloid shelf. *The New York Times* covers us regularly. We sometimes take for granted that the *Times* has nine million readers.

JM: **And they have more readers than anybody but the *Wall Street Journal*.**

ED: There was a great piece there on us and the ICA by Ada Louise Huxtable recently.

JM: **Has the fact that you are a couple created any confusion. I noticed that this year, for the first time, the Pritzker was awarded to two people – Herzog & de Meuron, a partnership.**

ED: Architecture has always valued the [lone] genius figure. There is definitely a change today. Collaborations are very much in the spirit of the times. Artists and architects are not as authorship-oriented as they were a decade ago.

JM: **Don't you think it's because so many woman entered the field, and gay partnerships are now accepted? So many of the best firms are**

composed of people in long-standing domestic partnerships.

ED: Certainly the fact that there is more diversity in architecture forces the public to accept an alternative to the heroic white male icon.

RS: The upside of being married is that we can be tougher with each other. The downside is that often you have to offer two for one ... like speaking engagements or even sharing a MacArthur.

JM: **I know the answer to this question, but it's important to ask it because of what a lot of architects believe. I assume you've never hired a publicist, have you? [Laughter all round]**

RS: We once wrote one into a play. We don't even have a business telephone listing! I would prefer not to look up and just do the work.

ED: It takes a long time to bring a body of work to the attention of the public but once you accomplish that, you produce an expectation that you will keep feeding the machine the same way. I remember when I was a student, John Hejduk was in the process of a radical departure from the course of his work. It got me very upset. Now that I am older, I understand.

RS: We like to be on shifting ground.

# Getting famous on Park Avenue

JM: If you were going to do one restaurant, the Brasserie was the place to do it. The Seagram Building has been a kind of launching pad. It introduced Mies in America; it gave Philip Johnson an entrée; it made Phyllis Lambert a patron as well as an architect. The building made modern architecture respectable in New York.

ED: The fact that it was an icon of modern architecture had a lot to do with our decision to take that project. We wanted to play with the presence and absence of Mies and Johnson. It was a space, when we first entered, of Mies's subconscious. By the way, Philip Johnson contacted us after his first visit. He said, 'I always knew you were smart, it's nice to see you put your intelligence into architecture.'

RS: There were a number of issues that interested us. The restaurant was in, perhaps, the greatest icon of 20th-century glass-and-steel architecture, yet it was situated inside of the one place in the entire building with no glass, the stone base ... the basement.

[The original interior had been destroyed by fire five years earlier.]

ED: That irony launched the project. We've done a lot of work on glass, glass and surveillance, glass and visuality. It fitted perfectly into our research. Our personal mandate was to rethink glass after modernism. [The restaurant has video cameras that record patrons arriving and then, after a slight delay, broadcasts the images on to monitors over the bar inside as they walk down the runway-like ramp into the space. This becomes the new grand entrance.]

RS: There was a waiter the other day who told us, 'It's the only restaurant I've ever worked in where architecture students come through on group tours.' ⌀

Jayne Merkel is Editor of *Oculus*.

# Life in the Afternoon

The Coach and Horses in Soho is perhaps the most famous London pub. Notorious in the 50s for the alcoholic excesses of the London Group – Francis Bacon and Lucian Freud – it was mythologised in the play *Jeffrey Bernard is Unwell*. A regular at the Coach and Horses, Paul Davies realised that on turning 40 he'd been involved in architectural education for over 20 years – drinking in the famous watering hole for many of them. Here, with photographs by Julie Cook, he evokes a day not unlike any of the others he has 'wasted' there, wondering why.

I once read that, before creating Disneyland, Walt Disney became fascinated by famous buildings. He visited The Empire State Building and wondered 'Why do so many people come here?' I suppose he developed some kind of criteria for it, a checklist perhaps, then went off and designed Disneyland. But what makes buildings famous (this includes the people who make them so) seems not to interest the architectural community. A student turning up at architectural school armed with sketches of Buckingham Palace (because it's famous) would soon find themselves diverted away to more interesting things.

Uncle Walt was no fool; he actually visited buildings and stood their thinking, 'what are people doing and why are they doing it?'

With this in mind I walked through the right hand door of The Coach and Horses, just as I had thousands of times before. 'The Coach' is a very famous pub. Of course, sitting in a bar is one of life's best experiences, which is why I do it so often. Drifting through the doors of the Coach and Horses in Soho to the gentle scent of stale beer, tobacco, and polish, marinating in sunbeams, at round about noon, is one of the loveliest things in the world.

At that time each day, the air is sublimely calm. There are just a few solitary drinkers, Norman ('London's Rudest Landlord') is playing patience, there are soft murmurs on the subject of illness and death, bodies soaking in to the day on the ancient patina of red vinyl seats. Soho is a late riser in the mornings, and the first mobile rings, like a wake up call, just past midday.

Gradually we drift in. We are essentially daytime, single drinkers (not those who arrive with friends or for a night out). We come because the Coach has qualities. An ex student of mine is first, enthusiastically brandishing his computer rendering of a vaguely wavy shape. We sit on the right, under the portrait of Jeffery Bernard.

Lunch is never respectably taken before 3pm, if at all. Regulars drift in and take their places on the stools at the bar, shuffling for the round, slightly higher variety. The first drunken artists of the afternoon sail through the door, to huddle argumentatively at a table. Talk meanders, intermittently between silences, across the bar. In dispute, history (drinkers are fastidious about history) is ammunition to be lobbed in great arcs, with passion. Pressing matters of local business are dealt with by the wheeler dealers over on the far (Greek St) side. London's Mayor pops in, to minor cheers. Then it's the paparazzi, on a two-day drunk after a scrum to shoot up the skirts of celebrities as they climb out of their taxis at The Ivy. In comes a professional gambler and two actors (one a lawyer in last week's Coronation Street, now Home Secretary in Othello) the other crippled in an accident, commuting in from a hostel in Peckham. Then the 'girls' (happy in pink Pringle sweaters perusing holiday brochures for Morocco) and a retired air force officer from Wembley. Here comes a distinguished real lawyer and Gordon, the architect, who once had his address as Soho Square (because that's where he was living- in the square). And of course there's Ian, who once 'worked' on 'The Lady'...then didn't, sipping Burton and Ginger beer, his frame racked by years spent here, or in 'the French', venally observing.

Age, sex, sexual orientation, race and rank, are irrelevant here. Political correctness is vilified. It makes you wonder what we're doing so wrong everywhere else. Moreover, while habitués of trendy Soho may think they're living, everyone in The Coach and Horses knows they're dying.

Norman barks at Julie and her camera, (until he realises he's already agreed to the shoot). It's his instinctive reaction to disturbance. Norman has become, pretty much, my bank manager. As Dan Farson wrote (amongst other things, like not being afraid to cry in public and seldom knowing the date) that a Soho person is someone:
'who cashes cheques anywhere, except the bank' and regards 'all brown envelopes with little windows as an unwarrantable intrusion'
So that's what we do.

These days, most of us commute to this place, to sit largely in silence, occasionally grunting with malicious conversation over the fine bitter sweet taste of a pint of Burton, or multiple Famous Grouse, drinking the heart out of the afternoon, watching the cigarette smoke curl to the ceiling. We congregate in particular parts of the pub. There are three entrances, and each habitually used by a certain group. To the right cynical professionals, bitter and twisted artists, hopeful actors, to the left, your traditional Soho types (some notable figures transcend both), in the middle the anonymous in no hurry to choose. Behind the bar there's Michael, there 25 years, in the company of a succession of transient bar staff whose chief characteristic is that they are visiting from abroad, so there for a shorter length of time than you, and entertaining in their command of English.

The Coach is the set for Keith Waterhouse's play *Jeffery Bernard is Unwell.* Jeff 'the perfect desirable wreck, the lightening conductor for bourgeois fantasies' first attracted me with a vodka soaked lecture at Bristol University solely on the subject of horses, women and suicide. Famous for his 'Low Life' column in *The Spectator,* cartoons from it, by Heath, line the walls.

Attracting tourists and wannabes, the place has the attributes of an English 'Cheers'.

Uniquely, in such a fast-moving world, The Coach and Horses has maintained a stoic resistance to change. Norman Balon, landlord for 45 years, has refused music, football, juke boxes, crisps, candles, gastronomy (other than the once famous dinners for his mum) stripped pine, souvenirs (other than match boxes and 'You're Barred you Bastard' mugs at Christmas) even toilets (they are 'maintained' in a state of notorious grime) or matching furniture. You may drink, read the paper (not books) and keep quiet if you haven't got anything to say. You may sing if drunk then get kicked out.

Around him, a maelstrom brews. *The Evening Standard* is outraged . Andrew Lloyd Webber complains at the syringes in the gutters and terrible public transport and carparking, putting theatregoers off. Local residents complain of drinkers puking on their doorsteps or worse. Crack dealers and Eastern European prostitutes are rife. Soho will have to be cleaned up.

In a cosmopolitan community for generations defined by small, individually let properties (ensuring diversity), one magnate, Paul Raymond, now dominates. As a consequence, perhaps, of fame, Denmark Street it's set to become the British pop music 'experience'. The '2i's' (pron: two eyes) 'Home of the Stars' (Georgie fame, Tommy Steele, Cliff Richard) the 'original' fifties coffee bar at 59 Old Compton Street is now a single bay in the giant 'Dome' café/bar. Coffee now floods the pavement as our demonstration of civilisation.

This change is inevitable, and some of it welcome.

piece, perpetually clean, with matching red vinyl stools, and no smoke curdling in sunbeams, while Charing Cross Road fills with Murder One bookshops, and other voyeuristic manifestations of our lives of crime?

We are no longer tolerant. But a careful look at the space where the Mayor of London mingles with the mob may be instructive. After all, it was designed, once, and once (I imagine in the late 60s) with the possibility of 'architecture as everything', pubs might have made a peep into the architecture studio as well as being an obligation at lunch. There are tangible, physical aspects, just as Disney would have observed; the patina of such intensely languid space, the shape and feel of the bar, the rail for holding on to, the height of the (different) stools, the tones, the decoration, the clock that's perennially five minutes fast. Of course he would reprocess it, cleaner, safer and extra large, but only because he understood the trajectory of our culture.

Pubs are an architectural blind spot, yet they are crucial to social life and to tourism. Architects may drink in them but we neither design them nor write about them . They are now a kind of embarrassing, sentimental subject in the thrusting world of competitive architecture. In the 90s, with all that interest in 'the everyday', I was hopeful. But all I got from this (renewed) interest in 'the everyday' was (surprise surprise!) the conjugation of ordinary materials in more 'interesting' ways.

Pub interiors are faux, the spatial arrangements awkward, the clientele unimpressed, and the activity dissipated. We soak there, one at each table, reading the paper, staring in to the mirror, a bunch of Walter Mitty's' living on borrowed dreams, but we EXIST! As a consequence, or perhaps a symptom, of a refusal to acknowledge the everyday, the Coach is a place where the subject of architects and architecture (in our land of wobbly bridges, fake porticos, giant gerkins and 'sustainable' office towers) is treated with the contempt it deserves.

I was pretty bitter and twisted that day.

Tutorials can be funny things in architectural school, and I had just given one that was very funny. Not that I was funny. I was simply in shock, hysterical, giddy with the kind of realisation that knocked 20 years in architectural education sideways.

A diploma student was trying to design a Bingo Hall. We were talking about entrances.
'So what are your first thoughts when you arrive outside your hotel on holiday?' I had asked, as some way of introducing the notion some sequence or other that might or might not be important.
Nothing.
'Relief?' I said, 'Nerves?' (paying the taxi?) I ventured, replaying such events over and over.
Nothing.
'Well what is the first thing you do once you're through

At least the sex shops become respectable. With all night shopping, with our need to keep theatres open, with the concerns of the local residents, there will be increased surveillance. But the technology of surveillance is the same as that which entertains us at home or on holiday. People will be excluded. For years the cosmopolitan centre of London, there are fears Soho will crackle with sniper fire of commercial competition, before capitulating to general trends. All Bar One's are inevitable.

I imagine, with Norman gone, the Coach and Horses as a heritage site, with a blue plaque. Maybe the graffiti on the Gents toilet door 'This toilet is no good for smokin' crack!' will be preserved for posterity, but I doubt it. Will 'The Coach' become some sort of museum

Above
Famous Grouse with ice.

the front door!?' I asked, encouragingly.
Silence.
'THE RECEPTIONIST!' I boomed
'Aarrrrrrrrrrrrrrrrrr!' (a twinkle of realisation)
'I need the key to my room! .....Then what do I
do?' I probed, wondering if this was my fault.
Nothing again (well actually a series of high
speed ummmings and arrrrings, accompanied
by glances at the ceiling)
'I go to my room!.... To get rid of my
baggage......and then what???'
    Nonplussed look.
I couldn't let this go on. I recounted the rituals
of hotel room arrival (putting on the television,
washing, unpacking, a little lie down etc)
to a blank face, as I began to realise the full
catastrophe of my predicament.
Then the killer. 'What do I do next?'
Utterly blank face, much rubbing of chin,
demur flickering of eyes, a little nervous laugh.

'I GO TO THE FUCKING BAR!!!!!!!!' I screamed, beside myself
with the realisation that this architecture student didn't
understand a word I was talking about.

So there it was. She might be able to bring me
morsels of glossy photographs of buildings she liked
the look of from magazines, but she hadn't got a clue
about what people do. She hadn't got a clue about how
to put this all together for people.

She did not understand the pleasures of an afternoon
sitting still in the Coach and Horses while our planet
speeds through space at 67,000 miles per hour. She did
not visit buildings and wonder at what people were
doing and why they were doing it. ⅅ

Paul Davies is an authority on the architecture of entertainment,
published in popular as well as academic journals including *Blueprint*,
*Bizarre*, *ⅅ*, *FX* and *Building Design*. He has lectured widely across
Europe and the USA. Julie Cook is a freelance photographer with a
background in the design industry. She has exhibited in London,
Liverpool and Bath and has published in many magazines including
*Bizarre, Sunday Times, ES Magazine, Blueprint*, *ⅅ* and *FX*. They can
be contacted via cook.davies@virgin.net

# Fame
## and Fortunes
## in Architectural Pedagogy

The phenomenon of fame, it seems, has become an integral part of contemporary architectural education. Jonathan Harris looks at the lecture and 'the crit' in their specific spatial settings as two sites of intellectual and professional reproduction. Observing the transmission of knowledge in the lecture theatre as being 'one-way' and seeing the crit as 'a theatre of linguistic and bodily exchanges', he examines the effects on the taught and on those who teach.

The ideal lecture theatre is vast, truly vast. It is a very sombre, very old amphitheatre, and very uncomfortable. The professor is lodged in his chair, which is raised high enough so that everyone can see him; there is no question that he might get down and pester you. You can hear him quite well, because he doesn't move. Only his mouth moves. Preferably he has white hair, a stiff neck and a Protestant air about him.
There are a great many students, and each is perfectly anonymous.
To reach the amphitheatre, you have to climb some stairs, and then, with the leather-lined doors closed behind you, the silence is absolute, every sound stifled; the walls rise very high, daubed with rough paintings in half-tones in which the moving silhouettes of various monsters can be detected. Everything adds to the impression of being in another world. So one speaks religiously.[1] *Bourdieu et al*

The world of pedagogy, for students of all kinds including those of architecture, is itself an architectural construction; so much, then, is clear. Pedagogy has various sites that share generic features of design and function. The lecture *theatre*, of course, in which the spectacle of the monologue is enacted: the transmission of 'knowledge', one way, top down, from the professor to the initiates. And the *studio*, in which the drama of 'communication' is usually located: the site for interaction, exchange, debate, 'crits', as well as of solitary student endeavour. In these physical, built spaces the work of intellectual and professional reproduction goes on: the fabrication of architects (in which students learn to identify with a pre-existing regime of authorities, ideas, practices and values), and the refabrication of architects (in which the professors confirm, ratify, revisit and reconstruct themselves as the 'experts').

Although the description at the start of this essay, of the experience a student had in attending lectures in Paris, comes from nearly 40 years ago, I do not believe it is out of date, despite '1968' and the attacks students made at that time on the educational establishments in western European and North American universities.[2] Nor do I believe that architectural students have ever had an experience that is fundamentally different from that of *all* students who are put through the institutions of higher education that are sponsored by the modern state in capitalist and self-proclaimed 'socialist' societies in the 20th century.[3] And students have also had to deal with, one way or another, the fame and repute of their teachers – though 'celebrity' and 'reputation' take many forms and universities mediate these forms within their specific pedagogic structures. In this essay I examine two of these – the lecture and the studio crit – and consider the transactions between professorial charisma, repute and architectural pedagogy.

## 1. Charismatics and the Ritual of the Monologue

Traditional teaching uses words to seduce. Through a process of osmosis, it promotes the transmission of an already confirmed and legitimate culture, and secures commitment to the values which this contains. Charismatic and traditional teaching stand in marked contrast to the rational use of language, which is suited to democratic education. The language of illusion in charismatic teaching can transmit only an illusion of its true value. In traditional teaching, the language of allusion presupposes a community of language between master and pupil and an already established complicity in values, and this occurs only when education is concerned with its own heirs.[4] *Bourdieu et al*

One kind of fame attaches itself to those professors who have the reputation for seducing students in various ways, including that done literally. (Malcolm Bradbury's notorious *History Man* is the 1970s fictional exemplar – 'leftist-sociologist' in Bradbury's liberal demonology, too clever by half to be morally defensible, though finally a not-to-be-pitied victim of his own seductive powers.) Sometimes real charismatic professors are famous for their architectural commissions as well – for *seductive design actions* in, and on, the 'real world', as it were, and for consequent media exposure of varying degrees – but this is not necessarily so. Academia is its own world as well as a fugitive subset of the wider one, and a kind of fame can easily be constructed and contained within the walls of the lecture theatre and the rhetoric of the studio crit. It may be fame and it may be notoriety: goodness and badness exist in equal proportion, the judgement depending on those judging. *Students*, as Bourdieu is at pains to argue, should not be seen, or see themselves, as epigones of their professors but rather as 'counterintuitive' sceptics (though very few ever become this). *Professors* measure their colleagues' performances in different terms: rivalry as academic communicators; in their understanding of how students should be 'treated' according to their broader social and political values; and as professionals if they 'practise' in that real world of buildings.

In the lecture theatre the naked authoritarianism of the pedagogic relationship is revealed and relished: the professor, actually or metaphorically on high, can say anything without literal contradiction. The student body is positioned as a receptacle of any and all gush, or is asleep, or talking, or 'texting', or absent. The lecture, therefore, is a ritual that mostly, and merely, confirms professorial authority and the power relations within the institution. Which is not to say that students don't listen, sometimes learn and occasionally are 'inspired'. But this is an inadvertent and mostly unintended consequence of the ritual. It is social roles that are really learnt, performed and reproduced in this theatre: the fame of the ineluctably boring lecturer as much as that of the astoundingly charismatic communicator – both denizens of academic teaching who prey on each other almost equally within the murky depths of departmental politics. The form of the lecture, however, is peculiarly appropriate to the rituals constituting *professionalisation* and the closures this process performs: architecture students are admitted to, and required to reproduce, what counts as expert knowledge and the values and behaviour which accompany it.[5]

### 2. Simulated Dialectics in the Studio

Under a system of teaching of the traditional type, which may include charismatic elements, the professorial function retains some features of the sacerdotal with which it was for a long time confused ... Views of teaching fall into two extreme categories: initiation into mysteries and infusion of grace, on the one hand, and impersonal communication of a particular body of knowledge on the other ... if one section of the student population inclines towards the researches of the intellectual master, the dominant concern for other students is scholastic effectiveness; or rather, nearly all students seem to equally and inconsistently share both expectations.[6]
*Bourdieu et al*

After a dip in the cold swimming pool, the heat of the sauna. Students are led to believe that the studio is the site for true exchange between themselves and their professors: an authentic synthesis of sorts. Crits are the coals that fuel this fire, and the papers lit to start it contain the 'project briefs' that are usually intended to motor students through their degrees. These briefs, brought down like tablets from the mountain, can be divided into Bourdieu's categories for types of teaching. Some are about initiation into the mysteries of 'good' or 'cutting edge' design practice, and thus are eccentric and mysterious in their own language. Students take them as seriously as they take the reputation of the professor's responsible for them. Others are based on the very limited, because essentially pragmatic, aim of meeting curriculum requirements that bodies such as RIBA set down: knowledge represented as required, fixed and final. Either the mysterious brief or the mundane one can lead to excellent or terrible results. The best students will always do well(ish), while the majority of the less able will drift and fall between the stools of meeting the impossible demands of the charismatic former and the possible but uninspiring demands of the professionalising latter.

The climax of studio life is the crit event itself: a theatre of linguistic and bodily exchanges between professors and students, carried on in front of the corpse of design work pinned to the wall. The visiting professor, *deux ex machina*, usually parachuted in again from the wider world of practice (famous for his or her real architectural achievements) bolsters the pedagogic apparatus in this moment of what is, for the student, quite apocalyptic judgement. However, what purports to be a genuine exchange usually ends up, in my experience, as a series of position statements from the experts met with a mixture of hurt feelings and misunderstanding from the students. The professors, of course, have relative linguistic command, fluency, bodily ease and professional reputation on their side – all facets of the rhetorical armoury learnt through years of involvement in these set-piece events. They also possess the hardness and *realpolitik* that is a product of their experience of business meetings with patrons of real buildings and development projects. My sense is that studio crits are actually nearly as ritualistic as the lecture form, though they include the performance

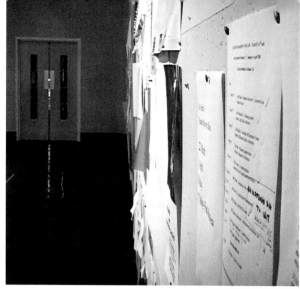

Notes
1. History student, female, aged 25, Paris, quoted in Pierre Bourdieu, Jean-Claude Passeron and Monique de Saint Martin, *Academic Discourse: Linguistic Misunderstanding and Professorial Power*, Polity Press (Cambridge), 1994, p 1. Originally published as *Rapport Pédagogique et Communication*, The Hague and the Ecole Pratique des Hautes Etudes, Mouton et Cie (Paris), 1965.
2. Alexander Cockburn and Robin Blackburn (eds) *Student Power: Problems, Diagnosis, Action*, Penguin/New Left Review (Harmondsworth), 1969); Paul Jacobs and Saul Landau, The New Radicals, Pelican (Harmondsworth), 1969; Trevor Pateman *Language, Truth, Politics*, Harvester (Brighton), 1978; and Jonathan Harris, 'Art education and cyber-edeology: beyond individualism and technological determinism', *Art Journal*, vol 56, no 3 (fall 1997), pp 39–45.
3. Mark Crinson and Jules Lubbock, *Architecture: Art or Profession? Three Hundred Years of Architectural Education in Britain*, Manchester University Press (Manchester), 1994.
4. Bourdieu *et al, op cit*, p 20.
5. Sociological accounts of the behaviour of architecture students are sadly lacking. An interesting parallel in fine art education was the ground-breaking study by Charles Madge and Barbara Weinberger carried out at the Lanchester Polytechnic, Coventry, in the 1970s: *Art Students Observed*, Faber (London), 1973.
6. Bourdieu *et al, op cit*, pp 106–7.

of remarks at various points, and on both sides, that are meant to indicate that both professors and students believe certain valuable things have been successfully communicated in the process. And sometimes they have been. But 'ritualistic', in its true linguistics sense, means redundant as a means of true communication. Professionalisation, on the other hand, has always had little or nothing to do with education in the fullest meaning that Bourdieu wishes to propagate.

'Fame' cannot be understood, then, in isolation from the differing fortunes of those implicated in the architectural pedagogic process. In minimal terms, to succeed as a student means merely to receive a good degree result, to pass exams, to be admitted to the professional ranks of those permitted to 'practise'. Charismatic professors help and hinder this process in a haphazard way. It is certainly true that students inveterately idealise certain architects and particular buildings and that these come to symbolise 'value' in some transcendent sense: that which should be emulated or aspired to, outside of the actual (and unrepeatable) specific set of circumstances in which a particular architect actually worked, or in which a particular building got designed and erected.

But this species of idealisation is only one of several which students internalise. Another, which is if anything more insidious and influential on student work, is that based on idealisations of society and history: that the former, for example, is a unity without contradiction, or that the latter, for example, is driven by value-free technological advances. Both assumptions feed into highly unrealistic and, I think, finally disabling notions of how the built environment got to be the way it is, and how change and 'progress' may be possible, and desirable, in design and construction processes. Perhaps what these forms of idealisation all share, and share

importantly with the media's usual representation of the work of architects, is a habit of radically abstracting and privileging different elements from what is actually a single process of production: be it the 'ideas' or 'visions' of an authorial designer, or of a feature in the material fabrication process, or a tendency in the wider social world. These are routinely fetishised, as in predominant accounts of modernism in architectural design – the 'genius of a lone creator' like Le Corbusier, the radical consequences of a particular material like concrete or glass, or the teleological Zeitgeist of 'planning and social democracy' in the 20th century. Let Ebenezer Howard and Lewis Mumford rest in their graves!

Architectural pedagogy finds it very hard to escape these conventions of thought, just as students find it very hard to escape 'the moving silhouettes of various monsters' haunting the lecture theatre and the studio crit. Unless architectural education is radically uncoupled from its role in the professionalisation process, in which the social type of the charismatic designer and 'intellectual master' has a structural part, Bourdieu's dream of a democratic education will remain unattainable. ⌀

Jonathan Harris teaches art and architectural history and theory in the School of Architecture at the University of Liverpool. He is author of *Federal Art and National Culture: The Politics of Identity in New Deal America* (Cambridge University Press, 1995) and *The New Art History: A Critical Introduction* (Routledge, 2001). The author would like to thank Oliver and Jane Linden for their helpful reading of an earlier version of this essay.

Reaching a wide international audience the British edition of *Vogue* can be regarded as a true barometer of fame – featuring those who are famous enough to be published, and published enough to be famous.

# Architecture in
# *Vogue*

Jamie Scott considers the way both architecture and architects are presented in this, the glossiest of fashion magazines, whose broad remit is to celebrate lifestyle as commodity. While such press coverage can often reduce architectural quality to the purely visual, Scott also demonstrates its beneficial effects as a source of positive publicity.

The desire of architects for recognition from their peers promotes an introverted condition of mutual admiration and self-congratulation within the profession. This is not always explicit to a wider public and often leaves those who commission and use architecture bemused. It is only the relationship between client and architect, however, that sustains traditional architectural practice. This essay considers one source of representation of architecture to a nonspecialist audience, and the concurrent development of a broader, publicly held, idea of architectural fame.

British *Vogue* is a fashion magazine with an annual circulation of around 190,000 – 10 times that of either the *Architects Journal* or the *Architectural Review*. Architecture and interior design are found across the full range of the magazine's content. Feature articles focusing on architecture define *Vogue*'s ethos towards the subject, whilst coverage extends to classified adverts which use the magazine to reach a particular target audience. Architecture also receives much coverage indirectly. Tourist destinations, new interiors in restaurant reviews and all manner of built environments for fashion shoots seem to suggest its ubiquitous quality as the backdrop to people's lives. Between 1990 and 2000 about 40 issues of *Vogue,* around a third published during that period, contained features concerned with architecture in some form.

In contrast to the architectural press, *Vogue*'s significantly different presentation of the subject to a large general readership is crucial to a public perception of architecture and the profession.

'This summer's swimwear is sleek, hi-tech and incredibly sexy. Grown-up, sensual looks incorporate graphic shapes and techno fabrics with no unnecessary flounces.'
So reads the introduction to a photographic feature on swimwear modelled in Peter Zumthor's spa baths in Switzerland.[2] The title of the article, 'Body Building', plays on the dual aspect of the feature. Replace the word 'swimwear' with 'architecture' and the sentence provides a parallel commentary to the images.

Without any reference to the architectural setting, this feature gives one of the most generous and direct expositions of a building to be found in *Vogue*. In all there are 11 full-page photographs and, apart from the vertiginous heels worn by the models, the compositions capture a resonant image of a building in use. The quality of the fashion photography is high, comparable to

any architectural photography, and the posed models give the building a scale and purpose sometimes lacking from dry architectural coverage. Where architectural photography depopulates the world to concentrate on pure uninterrupted form, these images remind us that human occupation, and use, is the origin of any building project.

Whilst the building has been widely published in, and is well known to, the architectural community, the discreet use of it in the shoot is perhaps closer in spirit to its 'quiet' style of architecture, a style which is often misrepresented by overexposure. Yet the strength of the architecture has clearly directed the composition and texture of each photograph and consequently dominates the atmosphere of the feature. The article exposes, and consequently conditions the reader to, an otherwise obscure architecture of the highest quality. The architect might be quietly pleased by the caption to one of the images, which offers an indirect appreciation of the building: 'The sleek structured lines of Eres's swimsuit make for a subtle sexiness that's entirely poised.'

It is the concern for the human and personal in *Vogue* features that distinguishes them from articles in the architectural media.

In a feature article on Zaha Hadid she is described as a 'revolutionary turned visionary' whose 'blueprints never conform to contemporary ideas for buildings'. A description of her style of work follows:

The term Deconstruction (a buzz word in fashion in recent years as clothes have loosened up and shown their seams) became an architectural label in the Eighties. As Deconstruction: a Student Guide points out, it was a period when very different architects in very different places put buildings – and bits of buildings – at odd angles so that they clashed and penetrated one another.[3]

The interest in Hadid is as a radical architect who can be seen to be continuing the 'high culture' of the Modern Movement. For *Vogue* this has associations with the glamorous intellectual activity of the first half of the 20th century. Photographs of the exterior of one of her buildings and her paintings, described as, 'all sexy curves and risqué zigzags', demonstrate the nature of the engagement. There is no comment regarding the purpose or content of her building designs.

Thus *Vogue* positions itself as a cultural commentator, picking up on the aspects of Hadid's work that connect to a broader realm of Modernism. The interest in Hadid is as a radical architect who can be seen to be continuing the 'high culture' of the Modern Movement. For *Vogue* this has associations with the glamorous intellectual activity of the first half of the 20th century. Photographs of the exterior of one of her buildings and her paintings, described as, 'all sexy curves and risqué zigzags', demonstrate the nature of the engagement. There is no comment regarding the purpose or content of her building designs. If publication validates the content of the article, then the reader is given the view that good architecture is primarily a visual subject which can be treated in similar ways to other fine arts.

The article moves on to the personal, describing Hadid's physique, and her wardrobe: 'She packs mass and volume into an Issey Miyake pleated jacket ...' The general profile that is created, mentioning family, friends, clothes and music as much as her architecture, is one of celebrity. It parallels any one of the feature articles common for more mainstream personalities. The status of *Vogue* allows it to promote whomever it chooses, and the nature of Hadid's architecture and her own flamboyance make her an appropriate subject. Her architecture shouts for attention and her significance as a female architect is deemed relevant in the readership of the magazine.

An article about Daniel Libeskind[4] presents a similar profile of another architect whose work again clamours for attention, and which duly receives it. *Vogue*'s interest in Libeskind was probably provoked by his extension to the Victoria & Albert Museum in London which must be the most famous unbuilt project in Britain, taking over the mantle from Hadid's Cardiff Bay Opera House.

Central to the article is the important supporting role of Libeskind's wife, Nina. It describes the key personal moments in the couple's careers, their family and nomadic lifestyle, all of which goes towards developing a public persona for Libeskind that is beyond the facelessness of other coverage. A profile of David Chipperfield[5] also discusses his private life, and notes that winning the commission to redesign the Neues Museum in Berlin was 'the watershed in his life'. It is the personal rather than professional in which the magazine is interested.

Along with personal profile articles there are more diverse features that demonstrate *Vogue*'s concern for the individual – a concern that generates a condition of fame. Lord Snowdon photographed six architects on a beach with self-built installations based on sand castles for a feature which the magazine concocted.[6] The images show John Pawson and Ron Arad, amongst others, posed alongside their sandy constructions with a short piece of text describing the surprisingly serious intentions of each design. The article serves as a piece of positive public relations for the architects, with full-page portraits and text that elaborates on their thinking and current projects.

The selection of the participants was dependent on their pre-existing cultural status, as we are given little contextual information other than that they are 'young British architects'. It is the images that dominate the article. The beach is a dramatic setting, the sand castles add spectacle and their transient nature gives the feature the quality of an event, a location in time. The posing of architects in this landscape is reminiscent of a fashion shoot and reflects a particular perception of the profession.

Quite what this perception may be is both crucial and subjective. Only male architects are featured. In the main, grown men in shorts building sand castles might offer an idea of independent wholesomeness. The exception to this is the Nigel Coates piece, in which Coates sits languidly next to his sculpture of the Thames which incorporates a male model lying flat on his back like some sort of homoerotic Lilliputian fantasy.

In a slightly more grounded article on the difficulties of sharing a home with somebody, the minimalist wishes of David Chipperfield are pitted against the storage requirements of his partner.[7] The feature begins with the author recounting her own move from a minimalist flat to the clutter and Victoriana of the home she shares with her new husband. It is telling that rather than the article being a reconsideration of the nature of domestic space, what is important to the writer is that each home was published, either in an exhibition at the RIBA or in a Habitat catalogue. It is exposition rather than argument that validates – Vogue's content is subsequently self-perpetuating.

Whilst the feature purports to explore the realities of sharing domestic space with a partner who has a different design sensibility, in actuality it ends up discussing the relationships of a series of architects and designers. It is a lifestyle article rather than architectural criticism, and probably more entertaining because of it. Chipperfield and his wife quibble over storage space in captioned photographs: 'Evelyn wants more cupboards in our house – I want the existing ones emptied.' Richard McCormack and his partner, interior decorator Jocasta Innes, give up entirely and live, like characters in a soap opera, in separate apartments with an interconnecting door. Each of the participants was obviously willing to reveal details about their private life, despite the article making little reference to their professional practice.

'The Glass Menagerie'[8] reviewed a house built by Future Systems, an architectural practice that is popular with Vogue. The article is a balanced piece that, unlike reviews of the same building in the architectural press, describes the house primarily from the point of view of the client. One of the attractions of the feature is that the occupiers are of suitable social standing to be of interest to the typical Vogue reader: the owner of a fashionable London restaurant and his television producer wife.

Of the eight photographs in the article, four contain members of the family. The main image depicts the husband behind the house in a racing green sports car, whilst the wife reclines on designer furniture in the garden. This gives

information by association, presenting the glamorous careers, smiling faces, car and house as combining into a lifestyle worthy of coverage. In the margin of the article there is a listing of all the objects displayed in the house, along with the name of the retailer. It seems the house and lifestyle have been hijacked to promote the consumable objects of interior design. The architecture becomes another consumable item: 'Roman blinds and steel mesh storage units by Future Systems. Bed linen and silk cushions from the Conran Shop ...'

The owners are clearly happy to have the publicity; the presentation of their home in the magazine validates and glamorises their choice and taste. Indeed, the very nature of the property, which is mostly glass, does not suggest introversion. As a lifestyle feature gives a view of a private realm, and makes what would otherwise be unknown desirable.

Vogue has little interest in the specific theories or motivations of architecture. Its concerns in reviewing design are twofold: appealing visual imagery which transfers successfully to the page; and the engagement of its readership. The magazine's readers are more interested in people than buildings, and it responds by making architects into celebrities.

The combination of articles, reviews and advertising presents numerous excerpts of lives, ideas and things. Vogue's ability to juxtapose isolated aspects of day-to-day life allows it to present a unified idea from complex, diverse elements. It collapses the difference between public and private, between commercial and cultural, and in so doing reduces previously separate conditions to the single quality of lifestyle.

In Vogue lifestyle is the commodity being offered, as showcased by the celebrities it features and promotes. Its connection to architecture is ignored by most specialist journals, but in our consumer society it can be a source of positive exposure for architects and their buildings. Lifestyle is to be acquired indirectly by the purchase of the suggested accessories, perhaps with architecture as the ultimate make-over.

It's easy to be dismissive of such representations of architecture, but the relationship of a magazine such as Vogue to its readership should not be undervalued. Modern architecture has been perceived to be prescriptive and paternalistic. By considering and engaging the public's aspirations and perception of design a more responsive architecture may be possible. ◬

Jamie Scott is currently working in the northwest England as site architect for a digital arts centre in Liverpool. Whilst his present concerns include the fine detail of the extension of time claims, his research interests centre on the condition of architecture in today's information-dominated society. A Liverpool School graduate, and occasional critic, he was previously involved with the European Architecture Students Assembly.

Notes
1. R Bowker (ed), Ulrich's International Periodical Directory 1997 (New Jersey), 35th edition, 1996.
2. N Niesewand, 'Body Building', Vogue (July 1998), pp 120–29.
3. Niesewand, 'Plane Speaking', Vogue (January 1994) p 102, pp 102–05.
4. Niesewand, 'Into the Lion's Den', Vogue (May, 1996), pp 238–41, 308.
5. Niesewand, 'Art and Craft', Vogue (April 1998), pp 204-9.
6. Niesewand, 'Nice Work If You Can Get It', Vogue (March 1993), p.202–7.
7. Niesewand, 'Home Truths', Vogue (May 1995) pp 134–7.
8. Niesewand, 'The Glass Menagerie', Vogue (October 1994), pp 204-10.

# Heinrich Klotz
# and Postmodernism
# in Germany

The first exhibition organised by Heinrich Klotz on the new premises of the Deutsche Architekturmuseum – a villa on Frankfurt's Schaumainkai converted by Oswald Mathias Ungers – took place in the summer of 1984 and featured the work of 34 international Postmodern architects. The exhibition was titled 'Die Revision der Moderne'. In spite of his reputation as a left-wing academic, Heinrich Klotz was made the museum's founding director by the conservative Frankfurt mayor Walter Wallmann in 1979. Torsten Schmiedeknecht investigates the role Heinrich Klotz and the Deutsche Architekturmuseum played in the public promotion of architectural culture in Germany in the 1980s and 1990s, with a focus on the rise and fall of Postmodern architecture.

This essay takes as a premise that any architectural canon and its establishment is dependent on the given society at a particular time in history that allows it to flourish.

Heinrich Klotz was born in 1935 in Worms, Germany, and died prematurely of cancer in Karlsruhe in 1999. At the age of 17 Klotz spent a year at the Santa Barbara High School in California and he retained close links with Anglo-American culture for the rest of his life. After having obtained a PhD in art history in 1963 and his habilitation in 1968, both from the University of Goettingen, he spent 1969 and 1970 as a guest professor at Yale University, and 1972 as a guest professor at Washington University, St Louis. Upon returning to Germany he became a professor at the Institute for Art History at the University of Marburg.

The person of Heinrich Klotz is inextricably linked to the development of Postmodern architecture in Germany and he used every possible medium to promote his vision of an architecture that, 'needs to be seen as a revision of modernism. My primary concern is to fully render the radical change that is tersely formulated in the precept "Not only function but fiction as well".'[1]

Klotz wrote and edited numerous books and articles, organised symposia, curated exhibitions and edited catalogues. He sat on juries for architecture competitions and was involved in local politics.[2] Although he was constantly opposed by the academic and professional establishment, he promoted architects like Venturi, Scott-Brown, Aldo Rossi and Charles Moore in Germany – he invited Venturi, Scott-Brown and Rossi to give their views at a symposium in Berlin in 1974 titled 'Gegen das Pathos des Funktionalismus' (Against the pathos of Functionalism).[3]

During his lifetime Heinrich Klotz was responsible for three major architectural endeavours in Germany: the redevelopment of the historic city centre of Marburg in the 1970s; the founding and running of the Deutsche Architekturmuseum in Frankfurt from 1979 until 1989; and the founding and managing of the Zentrum für Kunst und Medientechnologie (ZKM) in Karlsruhe from 1989 until 1998. He involved internationally renowned architects in all of these, providing some of them with

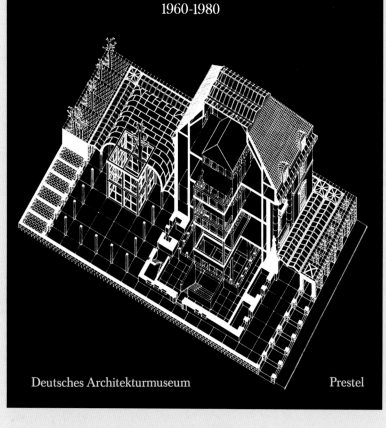

## Notes

1. Heinrich Klotz, *The History of Postmodern Architecture*, The MIT Press (Cambridge, MA), 1988, preface.
2. A few examples of his activities include organising a student protest against the demolition of a historic stable in Goettingen in 1966 (without success) and his successful work in the mid-1970s against the demolition of historic timber-frame buildings in Marburg's city centre.
3. Aldo Rossi later built a number of projects in Berlin.
4. Due to financial difficulties Koolhaas' project was abandoned and a new competition for a building on the site of an existing arsenal was organised. It was won by the Hamburg-based practice of Schweger and Partner who subsequently executed the conversion of the arsenal into the ZKM. The ZKM was officially opened on 18 October 1997.
5. Klotz, 'Der Fall Oswald Mathias Ungers', *Deutsche Bauzeitung*, 10 (1979), pp 15–17.
6. Five years later the Deutsche Architekturmuseum opened its doors to the public in the villa on Schaumainkai which had been converted by Ungers.
7. Klotz, 'Postmoderne' in Heinrich Klotz (ed), *Jahrbuch für Architektur 1980–1981*, Friedr.Vieweg & Sohn (Braunschweig/Wiesbaden), 1980, p 7 (translation T Schmiedeknecht).
8. Even though Klotz never managed to get Robert Venturi any work in Germany he was instrumental in promoting Venturi's ideas there. One has to remember that in the 1970s German mainstream architecture was still deeply

their first opportunity to participate in cultural architectural projects in Germany. In Marburg he worked with James Stirling, Charles Moore and Oswald Mathias Ungers, in Frankfurt he was responsible for commissioning Ungers as the architect for the Architekturmuseum and he played a pivotal role in the original invited competition for the ZKM in Karlsruhe in 1989, which was won by Rem Koolhaas. Klotz was highly influential in the decision to commission Koolhaas – who at that time had very little built work in his portfolio – for the project. The ZKM would have been Koolhaas' first major building in Germany and, like his entry for the Bibliothèque de France in Paris in the same year, the design for the ZKM was widely published and used to circulate Koolhaas' design philosophy.[4]

Heinrich Klotz chose his protégés carefully and once he had declared his support for an architect or artist he was extremely loyal in trying to get commissions and projects for the chosen one. It is probably no coincidence that in 1979, the year when he became founding director of the Deutsche Architekturmuseum (a job which included starting a collection and also establishing the new premises), Klotz wrote an article in the *Deutsche Bauzeitung* titled 'Der Fall Oswald Mathias Ungers' (The case of Oswald Mathias Ungers).[5] In it he fought on behalf of Ungers who had been the victim of a lot of criticism in the German architectural press in the late1970s. Klotz's analysis was that the architectural establishment had first attacked Ungers for his ideas about urbanism and architecture and was now copying him, but unfortunately without Ungers' talent and skills. According to Klotz, while Ungers was left with unfounded blame for 'his antics of decoration', his erstwhile critics were busy trying to outdo him by his own means.[6] In various publications Klotz always made it very clear who he was backing: 'There is a difference between the Florida hotels of Morris Lapidus and the buildings of Robert Venturi. It is a blind criticism that lashes out at Lapidus and is aimed at Venturi. It is a blind criticism that castigates eclecticism and tries to undermine Ungers or Rossi.'[7]

Apart from his direct involvement with, and lobbying for, specific architects, Klotz also had a major impact on

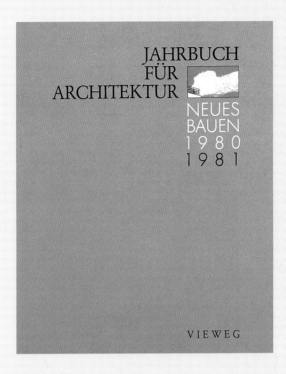

THE LANGUAGE OF
**POST-MODERN ARCHITECTURE**
CHARLES JENCKS

**THE FOURTH EDITION**

the development of mainstream architecture.[8] His version of the Postmodern canon in Germany is evident in his writings and publications and the exhibitions he curated in the late 1970s and early 1980s.

In 1980 Klotz started to edit the series *Jahrbuch für Architektur* for the Architekturmuseum. The first issue featured, amongst other projects, ones by Hans Hollein and Robert Venturi and included drawings of Ungers' project for the Architekturmuseum.[9] But Klotz also competed for his own claim to the rights of the story of Postmodern architecture. The Jahrbuch included an essay by him titled 'Post-Moderne?'[10] in which he tried to differentiate his idea of Postmodernism from that of Charles Jencks, whom he accused of promoting an 'anything goes' attitude resulting in a 'liquorice all-sorts' of architecture. In the introduction of his seminal book *The History of Postmodern Architecture*[11] there are no less than six mentions of Charles Jencks, whom Klotz had identified as his main rival for the throne of the guru of the history of postmodern architecture.

The book *The History of Postmodern Architecture* was first published in German under the title *Moderne - Postmoderne. Architektur der Gegenwart, 1960–1980* (Modernism and Postmodernism – architecture of the present) in 1984.[12] The title of the English version, published in 1988, is therefore not a direct translation from the German – perhaps it

was Klotz's late but definite answer to Charles Jencks' *The Language of Postmodern Architecture*[13] and emphasises Klotz' theory that Postmodernism is to be seen as a progression from modernism.[14] The late publication of the English version corresponded with the end of Postmodernism as Klotz saw it, and gave the book some authority as a historical survey of a past movement. The 1984 German version can be seen as having been aimed at the architectural profession in Germany, and was part of Klotz' quest to reinforce the production there of what he understood to be Postmodern architecture.[15]

Until the publication of *The History of Postmodern Architecture* Klotz had made his name internationally mainly as a curator, enabler and facilitator rather than as a theorist on contemporary architecture. *The History of Postmodern Architecture* was his first major English publication. It put him on the map as an internationally renowned critic of contemporary architectural matters and, in his role as director of the Architekturmuseum and later of the ZKM, probably added to his credibility so far as the funding bodies, sponsors, architects and artists he approached for exhibitions were concerned.[16]

The publication of *Moderne – Postmoderne* coincided with the first major exhibition Klotz curated in the new Architekturmuseum. 'Die Revision der Moderne' ran from 1 June 1984 to 10 October 1984 and was accompanied by a catalogue with the same title.[17] The architects it featured included Frank Gehry, Michael Graves, Hans Hollein, Helmut Jahn, Leon and Rob Krier, Charles Moore, Office for Metropolitan Architecture, Aldo Rossi, SITE, Oswald Mathias Ungers

rooted in its own version of the modernist canon which had been appropriated by commercial Functionalism. 'Abstraction' was still the rule, and anybody like Robert Venturi who proposed to look at the everyday in order to formulate an architecture based on signs and symbols that were accessible to the man in the street ran the risk of harsh criticism that verged on defamation.

9. Klotz (ed), *Jahrbuch für Architektur 1980–1981, op cit.*

10. Klotz, 'Postmoderne', *op cit*, pp 7-9

11. Klotz, *The History of Postmodern Architecture, op cit.*

12. Klotz, *Moderne - Postmoderne. Architektur der Gegenwart*, 1960–1980, Vieweg (Wiesbaden), 1984.

13. Charles Jencks, *The Language of Postmodern Architecture*, Academy Editions, (London), first edition 1977.

14. This is in contradiction to Jencks' postulation that there was a break between Postmodernism and modernism, expressed in his declaration that the death of modernism came with the demolition of the Pruitt Igoe housing estate in St Louis.

15. The publication of the English version cannot possibly have been aimed at such an audience. At the time the architectural establishment in most other European countries – particularly Britain – and in the United States had welcomed Postmodernism with open arms. In America people like Charles Moore, Michael Graves, Stanley Tigerman, Helmut Jahn and the group SITE had already established Postmodern thinking in architecture and thus had achieved what Klotz was trying to promote in Germany.

16. *Conversations with Architects*, which Klotz edited with John W Cook, had been published in 1973 and *Die Revision der Moderne* had been published as *Postmodern Visions* in 1985. However, *The History of Postmodern Architecture* was Klotz' first major publication as sole author.

17. Klotz (ed), *Die Revision der Moderne*, DAM und Prestel (Munich), 1984.

18. Klotz (ed) and Redaktion Andrea Gleiniger-Neumann, Hans-Peter Schwarz, *Bauen Heute, Architektur der Gegenwart in der Bundesrepublik Deutschland*, DAM und Ernst Klett Verlag (location), 1985.

19. The idea of an architecture museum in Germany dates back to 1906 when 37 architect

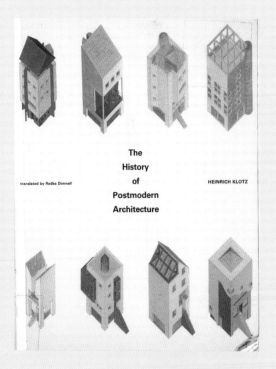

The
History
of
Postmodern
Architecture

translated by Radka Donnell

HEINRICH KLOTZ

**Bauen heute**
Architektur der Gegenwart
in der Bundesrepublik Deutschland

Deutsches Architekturmuseum Frankfurt a. M.

and Robert Venturi. Klotz' introduction to the catalogue reads like a homage to his all-time favourites: Moore, Rossi, Venturi and Ungers. An equivalent exhibition to ' Die Revision der Moderne' concerned German architecture and followed in the summer of 1985. 'Bauen Heute' (Building today), also manifested in book form, was a major retrospective showing a cross section of Postmodern architectural activities in Germany since the early 1980s.[18]

The value of the Architekturmuseum for the careers of a number of German architects was immense. For the first time in the history of Germany there was an institution dedicated to promoting contemporary architecture and – most importantly – architects.[19] Whereas 'Die Revision der Moderne' had been an account of international tendencies in Postmodernism, 'Bauen Heute' featured, apart from already established German architects, a significant number of the country's newcomers and was launched as a representative survey of contemporary architecture in Germany. Although its title was 'Building today', some practices like Kollhoff Ovaska made it into the exhibition without showing a single built project. Other young practices that were featured were Frankfurt-based Berghof Landes Rang – who at the time were riding high on the wave of decorative Postmodernism[20] – Eisele und Fritz, Christop Maeckler and Bangert, Jansen, Scholz und Schultes who had won the competition for the Schirn Museum in Frankfurt.[21]

None of the above made it on to the list of Heinrich Klotz' all-time greats. In his autobiography, *Weitergegeben* (Passed on), which was published after his untimely death in 1999, Klotz dedicated a whole chapter to seven architects whom he highly respected.[22] His account of his relationships with them is interesting in that it reveals that he respected them not only for their work but – in some cases probably even more – for their personalities. The seven architects featured in the chapter called 'Meine Helden' (My heroes) are Oswald Mathias Ungers, Paul Schneider-Esleben, Aldo Rossi, Hans Hollein, Robert Venturi, Charles Moore and Rem Koolhaas.

'Bauen Heute' showed the work of 64 – mostly German – architects.[23] In his introduction to the 'Bauen Heute' catalogue Klotz explained that some architects had been deliberately ignored for the exhibition because they had either been part of 'Die Revision der Moderne', like Ungers or, like Guenter Behnisch, their work was planned to be shown in 'Vision der Moderne' which was to follow in 1986. Incidentally, in the catalogue for 'Vision der Moderne'[24] Behnisch (who was one of the most successful German architects in the 1960s and 1970s, but also a fierce critic of some of Klotz' protégés like Stirling and Ungers) would not feature with a single building other than the Olympic Stadium in Munich, the concept of which many critics credited to Frei Otto.[25]

Klotz' vision, and his constant promotion of the work of architects like Ungers and Rossi, has left its mark on the German architectural landscape. His work as a chronicler of contemporary architecture has helped to open the door for some developments (like Deconstructivism) and to sustain others (like analogue and contextual architecture).

and engineer organisations
started work on a manifesto
which was completed in 1913.
The project was abandoned
because of the First World
War. See Klotz's essay 'Das
Deutsche Architekturmuseum
in Frankfurt am Main',
*Jahrbuch für Architektur
1980–1981, op cit*, p179.
**20.** Incidentally, in line with
contemporary 'good taste',
Landes has just completed a
mixed-use building in
Frankfurt reminiscent of
Hilbersheimer.
**21.** Schultes – together with
Charlotte Frank – is the
architect for the new
government buildings in
Berlin.
**22.** Klotz, *Weitergegeben*,
DuMont (Cologne), 1999.
**23.** From March to June 2000
the exhibition 'Germany',
subtitled 'Mensch und Raum'
(Man and space) ran as part of
the Architecture in the 20th
century series in the
Architekturmuseum, under the
directorship of Wilfried Wang.
Amongst the more than 70
architects whose work across
the 20th century was shown,
there were five who had been
part of 'Bauen Heute': Heinz
Bienefeld, Hans Kollhoff, Axel
Schultes, Otto Steidle and and
the practice of von
Gerkan/Marg und Partner.
**24.** Klotz (ed) and Volker
Fischer, Andrea Gleiniger-
Neumann, Hans-Peter
Schwarz. *Vision der Moderne.
Das Prinzip Konstruktion*,
DAMund Prestel (Frankfurt and
Munich), 1986.
**25.** Interestingly, Frei Otto,
famous for his pioneering
engineering work on tensile
structures, had a number of
projects in the exhibition and
features prominently in the
catalogue.
**26.** Klotz, *Architektur der
Zweiten Moderne*, DVA
(Stuttgart), 1999.
**27.** *Ibid*, pp 14–15 (translation
T Schmiedeknecht).
**28.** Germany has not yet seen
the development of an
architectural elite, as has
happened in Britain where
some architects have achieved
celebrity status and are
accepted by the political
establishment, the public and
the profession as the chosen
few who seem to be the only
possible choice to design
buildings of major public and
cultural interest. This status is
at times exploited by the stars
to exert pressure and defend
their British hunting grounds
while, at the same time, some
of the most celebrated British
architects rely heavily on
commissions from abroad.
**29.** The Deutsche
Architekturmuseum is currently
under the directorship of Dr
Ingeborg Flagge.

**Heinrich
Klotz**

**Architektur
der
Zweiten
Moderne**

**Ein Essay
zur Ankündigung
des Neuen**

**DVA**

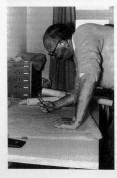
By the middle of the 1990s the popular architectural style in Germany had shifted from the decorative and the representational to what Klotz shortly before his death postulated as the beginning of 'die Zweite Moderne' (the second modernism). In *Architektur der Zweiten Moderne*[26] Klotz describes how he sees contemporary architecture moving away from the decorative and the illustrated narrative in order to reconnect with, and continue, the unfinished project of the modernist avant-garde of the start of the 20th century:

> The era of Postmodernism that began around 1965 and had been dominant in the years between 1970 and 1990, is fading. Whereas in Postmodernism the spearhead of thinking and designing had been aimed against a degenerate modernism and had become a revisionist corrective, the best examples of today's architecture refer to the early modernist tradition of the 'Neues Bauen' and take inspirations from its roots in order to continue the 'unfinished project of modernism' and to give it new strength.[27]

The projects of six contemporary architects are illustrated in the small booklet: those of Peter Kulka, Oswald Mathias Ungers, Guenter Behnisch, Daniel Libeskind, Zaha Hadid and Frank Gehry.

It is not only the start of the 21st century that has seen the celebration of a subject often leading to the celebration of the personalities involved with it.[28] And the questions in connection with the promotion and representation of architecture in different media remains the same – whether quality will always rise to the top and whose idea of quality is represented. Or is architecture, and for that matter are architects, like most commodities, also largely dependent on social, political, economical and cultural circumstances and the skills and contacts of makers and promoters?

Heinrich Klotz was not an architect or a designer, but his name and his work in the field of architecture is manifest in many buildings designed by architects whom he enabled, encouraged and supported. Two major cultural institutions remain as his legacy: the Deutsche Architekturmuseum in Frankfurt, a unique place in which the culture of architecture and architects is celebrated; and the Zentrum für Kunst und Medientechnologie in Karlsruhe.[29]

The story of Heinrich Klotz is that of one man's crusade to promote his belief in the power of architecture. Often swimming against the tide and fighting the conventions of the 'good taste' of the architectural establishment, his choices were often unpopular. But in his lifetime he was one of the most powerful shapers of tastes, opinions and architectural styles in Germany. His understanding of, and skills in using, cultural institutions, politics and the media to promote his ideas often enabled him to make the exception the norm. ⌀

Torsten Schmiedeknecht is an architect. He is currently a lecturer in architecture at the School of Architecture and Building Engineering, University of Liverpool, where he is the Director of Studies for the BArch course.

Above
Klotz with his heroes – Oswald Matthias Ungers, Charles Moore and Aldo Rossi with Klotz – as illustrated in his autobiography *Weitergegeben*.

Previous spread
The cover of Klotz' *Architektur der Zweiten Moderne*.

# Fables of
# Visibility

## Architect and Photographer: a Critical Bond

Since the first decades of the 20th century the photographic image has been the primary means of communicating architecture to its public. Pierluigi Serraino assesses the relationship between architecture and photography, and, in turn, between architect and photographer. Considering the role of photography within a broader cooperative enterprise, which involves every cog in the media and its sale, Serraino supports his argument with rarely seen works of the renowned architectural photographer Julius Shulman.

Can there be a famous modern building without a famous photograph? Would architects achieve the foreground of collective visibility without the photographic representation of their built work? Scores of illustrations inhabit the popular and specialised press to celebrate the portfolio of an exclusive league of designers. Occasionally, it happens that one image is so ubiquitous in the pages of mainstream literature that it becomes the definitive statement of the project it is intended to portray: the window walls of Walter Gropius' Bauhaus in Dessau, Germany, photographed by Lucia Moholy; Man Ray's rendition of the triangular balconies of Harwell Hamilton Harris' Weston Havens House in Berkeley, California; the bricolage of architectural orders of Charles Moore's Piazza d'Italia in New Orleans, Louisiana, captured by Norman McGrath; the bathers in Rem Koolhaas' Villa Dall'Ava in Saint-Cloud, Paris, choreographed by Peter Aaron of the ESTO agency, are a few notable cases among many from our distant and recent past.

Yet, architectural photography is a fairly recent acquisition in the production of design discourse. Ever since its introduction in the world of publications, pictures and their authors have progressively acquired a central position in the construction of consensus and fame for architects. If blueprints are bearers of meaning in the restricted circle of specialists, photographs capitalise on a universal code that makes them a primary vehicle of communication between architects and the general audience. Hardly documentary, pictures affect the perception of the work portray, as they both reflect and direct common beliefs about space in the time when the snapshots are taken.[1] In addition, photography is the viable avenue to vicariously extend the architectural experience of an artefact to those who are unable to access the site. William Hedrich's 1937 canonical shot of Fallingwater is still for most people their sole opportunity to visually consume Frank Lloyd Wright's milestone, since only the lucky few are able to reach Bear Run, Pennsylvania, where the residence is built. Therefore architecture nowadays relies heavily on photographic representation for its large-scale circulation and public assessment beyond its finite geographical coordinates and disciplinary boundaries. Photography is the ultimate chance for a built statement to be permanently traced in the map of architectural achievements.

But to photograph buildings as a subset

practice in artistic investigations and to practise full-time architectural photography as a profession with commercial purposes are indeed two separate activities. The former constitutes a set of keen observations within the production of art photographers who are interested in making critical pictorial statements over a wide range of themes;[2] the latter is an occupational speciality in its own right, whose influence attained its full thrust in the 1930s. It was around that time, and especially in the United States, that architectural photography shifted from being documentary of the human-made environment to being celebratory of modernity as a new age of progress. The Hedrich brothers (Ken, Ed and Bill), Julius Shulman and Ezra Stoller entered the professional scene between 1929 and 1939.[3] Together with a narrow group of photographers throughout North America, they focused their lens almost exclusively on modern structures, marketing their skills and services in the architectural profession, building industry and the media. At that critical juncture, authorship in architectural photography started becoming a factor in the appreciation of what was depicted in the black-and-white print. More and more buildings were captured in definitive photographs in those years, bestowing an aura to them and to the époque, while increasing the cultural 'stocks' of the architect. Occasionally, the fame of those images reached such an extreme that whether the architecture or the photography should be credited became a point of confusion.

There is a definite correlation between
the renown of the modernist architect
and a particular photographer

There is a definite correlation between the
renown of the modernist architect and a
particular photographer. Long-term alliances
between these two parties have traditionally
scripted historical accounts in the discipline:
Richard Neutra and Julius Shulman, Richard
Meier and Ezra Stoller, Paul Rudolph and Joseph
Molitor, Craig Ellwood and Marvin Rand, Tadao
Ando and Yukio Futagawa are some of the known
pairs in the visual gallery of modern
architecture. Since to photograph is to interpret,
a long-lasting relationship between these two
agents grants the work of a particular architect
consistency as well as homogeneity of pictorial
representation, suggestive of a coherent and
linear development in the production of his or
her design statement. The triad of architect,
photographer and building forms the core unit
towards the creation of architectural distinction.

Photographers also make their living selling
pictures. They do so through the network of
personal connections built up during years of
practice with the publishing world, especially

with editors.[5] For an architect, hiring a photographer
means buying the skills for pictorial reproduction and
gaining access to the exclusive circuit of the mass
media. Looking for exposure to market their built
endeavours in magazines, designers court acclaimed
icon creators in order to have their work captured on
film. This dynamic automatically puts photographers in
touch with the latest accomplishments that are still
unfamiliar to the community at large and makes them
ideal key informants for publishers. They therefore
bridge the gap between the architectural profession and
the popular and professional press. By default, they
become active promoters/agents of architects and
primary consultants for editors in search of new design
talents. This pattern of discovery applies to many of the
clients of Julius Shulman.

A case in point is the Chicken Prairie House, also
known as the Greene Residence, designed by Herb
Greene in 1960. When the house was built it received
great exposure in the press. Its first public appearance
in the Better Living section of *Life* magazine opened a
host of editorial opportunities to the young architect.
The building's bird-like look and the collage
arrangement of the shingles induced the author of the
article to compare the artefact to a prairie chicken and
raised the curiosity of the press worldwide. Shulman
had been in the neighborhood of the Greene Residence
to photograph Bruce Goff's Bavinger House for *Horizon*
magazine. He also visited Greene's first structure, still
unfinished, and decided to take pictures of it. When he
showed the photographic material to the editors of *Life*
in New York they scheduled its publication a month
later on 24 November 1961.

Shulman's personal connections with Progressive
Architecture resulted in a six-page review of the
residence in that magazine the following year. It
included nine photographs, a few construction drawings
and descriptive text. Along with the *Life* article, this
generated a chain reaction in the media. Shulman's
pictures popped up in national and international
architectural magazines. After the completion of the
residence in 1963 John Peters covered it in the food
section of *Look* with new images by a different
photographer. Four years later, *House Beautiful*
included the house on a cover story about wood
shingles. In later years, surveys of American
architecture continued to include the residence as an
example of a unique elaboration of the organic
principles defined by Frank Lloyd Wright.

Located on 48th Avenue between Robinson and
Alameda, four miles east of Norman, Oklahoma, with no
neighbouring houses within half a mile, the Greene
Residence was in territory unfamiliar to photographers.
Approximately 2,100 square feet in size, two storeys
high and costing a total of $25,000, the organisation
of its functions was relatively conventional. Yet its

Opposite
Raul Gardrund, James Toland
Residence, San Clemente,
California, 1967

Above
Carl Maston, Thies Residence,
Los Angeles, 1962

Notes
1. Thomas Fisher, 'Imagine
Building', in *Progressive
Architecture*, August 1990, p 94.
2. Cervin Robinson,
*Architecture transforemd: a
history of the photography of
buildings from 1839 to the
present*, Cambridge, MA. MIT
Press, 1987, p 110.
3. Julius Shulman,
*Photographing architecture and
interiors*, Los Angeles: Balcony
Press, (reprint) 2000.

volumetric development was a radical departure from mainstream design propositions for domestic space. Behind the elliptical shape of the house lay the intent to deflect the storm winds of the prairie. The exterior of the residence evoked images of birds, shelter, mythological creatures, dens and the like. Interiors and exteriors were blended through the singular use of shingles, a metaphor for feathers, which covered the walls evenly inside and outside. Greene lived in the house with his family for three years before moving to a different location.

This unprecedented design, which emerged from Greene's view of organic architecture, appealed to editors of popular magazines as well as to those of architectural journals. Adjectives like 'wildly different', 'fantastic', and 'wacky' were sprinkled throughout the article in *Life*. *Progressive Architecture*, instead, presented the Greene Residence as the outcome of a conceptual process, the roots of which go back to Frank Lloyd Wright, Bruce Goff and Antonio Gaudí. Such a widespread consensus opened the doors for the architect to achieve a more

permanent position in architectural history books. The highly personal gesture of the Greene Residence had a strong bearing on self-built housing in the late 1960s, and on the development of a new vernacular vocabulary in the Midwestern regions of the United States. Shulman's involvement was pivotal for the visibility of the architect's early work. As a young designer Greene was hardly in the position to launch his unconventional house into the limelight of the media attention. It was the Californian photographer who did the work for him.[5]

Nonetheless, the partnership between architects and photographers has to be seen within a wider consideration about architecture and public relations. When these fail to work concurrently, the toll architects pay is that they disappear from the authoritative accounts of the domain. The case of Rudolph Schindler is paradigmatic in this respect. He was born and died in the same years as Erich Mendelsohn (1887 and 1953). At the time of his death Schindler, almost forgotten, received an obituary in *Arts & Architecture*,[6] but no mention in the rest of the press. Mendelsohn, on the other hand, was commemorated with large coverage in all the major tabloids of the time. Schindler was virtually erased from the written history of architecture. Only seven years later, through the research efforts of

attention of the reader; it triggers the interest of the design community in a specific project and works as a catalyst for collective attention and recognition. It further helps to single out the architect's name from the stream of images that flood the publishing industry, but ultimately it is only a starting point in activating the promotional machine on a global scale that has delivered the master builders to us. A cultural and social infrastructure is needed for a built statement to be seen as being archetypical of its own time. This explains why architects of the calibre of William Sutherland Beckett, Whitney Smith and Wayne Williams, Kenneth Lind, Mario Ciampi and many more have been excluded from books about architecture. Despite having Shulman photographing their projects and so gaining temporary recognition, they lacked the long-term commitment of an editorial sponsorship and the institutional endorsement of the establishment, which would have been necessary to secure their work in architectural history.

The bond between architect and photographer is still a current variable in the equation of fame. The Guggenheim Museum in Bilbao, Spain, designed by Frank Gehry, is undoubtedly known as an architectural event worldwide. But only a fraction of those who are aware of the museum's existence actually get to Bilbao to experience the space. The rest formulate a position about it through the exposures of Jeff Goldberg/ESTO. More recently, Craig Hartman/SOM counts on Timothy Hursley's dusk shot of the sweeping trusses of the roof structure to generate a positive reception of his new San Francisco International Terminal by the global readership.[8] Architectural photography is nowadays a far more competitive field than it was when Julius Shulman started in 1936. Then, he remembers, five or six photographers in the United States concentrated exclusively on architecture. Today dozens of photographers populate the professional scene in America, in Europe and Japan. Architects still crave for that definitive eye-stopper to make a case about their work. For those living in the shadows of their famed colleagues, and for those who didn't, don't and will not make it in books and in a collective approval of their design, the photographs provide clues to their dedication and commitment to the world of architecture. ⌀

A practising architect with a keen interest in the history of his profession, Pierluigi Serraino graduated from La Sapienza, the School of Architecture of the University of Rome, in 1994. He earned his MArch at the Southern California Institute of Architecture (SCI-Arc) in Los Angeles in 1996, and his MA in architecture at the UCLA in 1999. His projects and writings have been published internationally in *Hunch*, *Space & Society*, *Global Architecture* and *Rassegna*, among other publications. Born in Messina, Italy, Serraino currently lives in San Francisco where he is practising the profession and working towards his PhD in architecture at UC Berkeley. He can be reached at serraino@uclink4.berkeley.edu.

4. Joseph W. Molitor, *Architectural photography*, New York: Wiley, 1976, p 148.
5. Julius Shulman, *Architecture and its Photography*, Koln: Taschen, 1998, pp 202-6.
6. Esther McCoy, 'Schindler Houses of the 1920s', in *Arts & Architecture*, September 1953 and 'Work of RM Schindler' in *Arts & Architecture*, May 1954.
7. William Marlin, introduction to *Nature near: the late essays of Richard Neutra*, by Richard Joseph Neutra, Santa Barbara, CA: Capra Press, 1989, p vii
8. 'The Ontology of the Photographic Image', in Andre Bazin, *What is cinema?*, Berkeley, University of California Press, 1967-71.

historian Esther McCoy, did he receive his first major acknowledgement as a pioneer in American modernism. That was the beginning of his cultural reconsideration. Neutra, on the other hand, was far more political in cultivating his relationships with publishers and in handling his image for media consumption.[7]

Fame in architecture is a cooperative enterprise. It takes an architect, a building, a photographer, a writer, a tabloid, an audience, a publisher, an editor, a distributor, a bookseller, a historian, a forum of exchange, a discourse around a period – and more – to construct the shared memory of architecture. A definitive photograph certainly commands the visual

'The Greatest Architect who will ever live'[1]

# Fame +
## Frank Lloyd Wright

Having understood the mechanics of self-publicity from a very early stage in his career, Frank Lloyd Wright was no stranger to the phenomenon of fame. Howard Martin looks at some of the methods employed by Wright in his pursuit to become – or remain – 'the greatest architect who will ever live'. Concluding that Wright saw himself as 'the heroic artist', Martin reveals that Wright's whole life was based on a strategy grounded in means and ends. Accordingly, if one considers oneself to be the best architect in the world, fame naturally becomes a necessity.

Sir Donald Bradman was the most famous cricketer of the 20th century. He was also the greatest. Previously the fame had gone to Dr WG Grace but so had the infamy. Fame and infamy, like notability and notoriety, are contraries rather than contradictories and Frank Lloyd Wright spectacularly combined all four in a career that overlapped those of both cricketers. Today, despite his notoriety, few architects, critics or interested laymen would deny Wright's pre-eminence as an architect, nor the quality of his architecture. Despite his blatant self-promotion, breathtaking arrogance, shameless mendacity, disregard or denigration of others, a personal life that defied American convention and was seen as irredeemably immoral, and an ability to alienate almost everyone he met (and many he didn't) he still features high in the pantheon of architects.

A characteristic of Wright's domestic buildings after the mid-1890s is a somewhat hidden entrance and a complex path to the central core of the house – which for Wright was the hearth – usually where the implied axes crossed. In the Bach House in Chicago (1915) there are no less than 11 turns to be made in the journey. The concealment of the entrance and the inaccessibility of the building's metaphorical heart suggests a connection with Wright's own personality that may shed some light on his less agreeable aspects – not as a straightforward parallel (keeping his true motives and inner self hidden from others, etc) but as a less conscious and therefore more informative key to his true self.

Wright's elaborately contrived appearance, behaviour, showmanship, organisation of accoutrements and entourage – what Brendan Gill refers to as his 'many masks'[2] – do not conceal his character. Even allowing for the levels of sophistication to which 'spin' has risen in recent times to protect the reputation of politicians and others, Wright stands out as a master. Or does he? What exactly was Wright spinning away? What image was he trying to create? What was he concealing about himself?

I would like to suggest that the answer to the last question is, surprisingly, nothing. He didn't refute any of his misdeeds though he didn't always interpret them in the same way as others did. He didn't honour his financial debts but he didn't deny them either. He didn't deny his height although he made himself taller in the eyes of the world and made a virtue of it when challenged, talking about human scale and the fact that a little height could go a long way in the

prairie.[3] He didn't claim to be a great thinker, even confessing in his autobiography that he had a laziness in that area and thought only when it was forced on him. He didn't claim modesty or humility: he revelled in his arrogance.

This arrogance goes far beyond what even he knew to be acceptable to most people. Yet he made no effort to disguise it. As he says in *The Future of Architecture*, 'early in life I had to choose between honest arrogance and hypocritical humility. I chose honest arrogance and have seen no reason to change it even now.'[4] The subtle trick here was to insert the word honest as an emotive adjective of universal approbation. He was less subtle when, arraigned for contravention of the Mann Act[5] in the 1920s, he was asked to state his occupation by the judge. His reply, 'I am the world's greatest architect', prompted his future wife Olgivanna to suggest to him later that evening that he had, perhaps, been rather immodest – to which he replied, 'But, my dear, I was under oath to tell the truth.'[6]

He can hardly have charmed one particular critic when he wrote in 1930: 'I warn Henry-Russell Hitchcock here and now that, having a good start, I intend to be not only the greatest architect of all time but the greatest who will ever live. And I do hereby affix the "red square" and sign my name to this warning.'[7] The red square in question was subsequently applied

**Above**
The red square with which Frank Lloyd Wright announced that he was the 'greatest architect who will ever be'.

**Opposite left**
Details of the inscriptions on Wright's grave. Wright changed both his given name – Frank Lincoln Wright – and his date of birth.

**Opposite right**
Frank Lloyd Wright's grave in Spring Green, Wisconsin, 1959.

**Overleaf**
Model of Broadacre City, Taliesin, Wisconsin, 1935. This model, built by Wright's apprentices to publish his utopian linear city, cost more than the completed Robie House.

retrospectively to earlier ones suggesting that Wright came to consider that his phrase 'intend to be' was too modest.

Since there could only be a single Number One architect, Wright no doubt felt he had to denigrate his rivals.They became 'Old Mies' (he was 20 years younger than Wright), 'Little Philip' (from the 5 foot 8 inch Frank Lloyd Wright), 'Three blind Mies' (SOM), Skiddings, Owe-more and Sterile (SOM again)[8] and so on. When he met Saarinen on Chicago Station in the 1920s and Saarinen asked him what he thought of his (Saarinen's) new building in Colombus, Wright replied: 'Well, Eliel, when I saw it I thought what a great architect – I am.' Wright relates this in his autobiography and goes on to say of the incident, 'that, I'm afraid is me. Saarinen was born and will die – a Finn ... I still refuse to die'.[9] Architects from the past were usually no less open to derision and those that escaped his acerbic tongue were treated as heralds of Wright himself. Even Jesus was dragged into the act, the tenuous connection being that he was a carpenter ('perhaps the architects of the day'[10]). Wright calls him the first organic architect.[11] Christ suffered on the cross for his crown and it would have been unlike Wright not to have felt that he had similarly suffered for his art.

The religious nexus is perhaps to be expected from someone with Wright's background. His ancestors were, by all accounts, garrulous Welsh windbags, some of them Unitarian preachers, and his father was a preacher for a period. When Frank's son John came to write about his father it is significant that he entitled his book *My Father Who Is on Earth*.[12] The Taliesin Fellowship[13] was run in a way very reminiscent

of a religious order with Wright's widow Olgivanna carrying on Wright's role after his death, as high priest(ess). Wright said he was influenced by Pythagoras, and the foundation seems more akin to a Pythagorean semireligious secret society (or, rather, society with secrets) than a Christian order. Wright, however, was not a prophet of God (nor, as many people might have thought, of himself) but rather a prophet of Architecture (his, of course, but only because his was the best) in the way that Pythagoras was a prophet of mathematics, a word he invented. Wright, for his part, could only add 'organic' to the existing word architecture.

Wright had said that architecture was nothing but the transformation of ideas into built form, and that no building had a right to be erected unless it was the working out of some idea,[14] so it is not surprising that he admitted Plato as one of his influences. In Plato's utopian *Republic* the ultimate aim of education was to produce the philosopher-king who would rule the state. In Wright's utopia, Broadacre City,[15] it is the architect-statesman who will organise society by designing its form and fabric.[16] Wright always saw himself as the heroic artist-architect and in this context he writes approvingly of Shelley and his views on the poet as the 'legislator of the world' – indeed, he uses the phrase as the title of a section of one of his books.[17] Carlyle's heroes Beethoven, Napoleon – Wright was particularly struck by the latter's comment, 'Do you know what amazes me more than anything else? The impotence of force to organise anything'[18] – and Nietzsche's superman are amongst the predictable creators from the past who found approval from Wright and whom he saw as his progenitors.[19]

The 'ordinary' people were unlikely to appreciate Wright referring to them as 'the herd' – a term he had taken from Carlyle – and he also coined the phrase

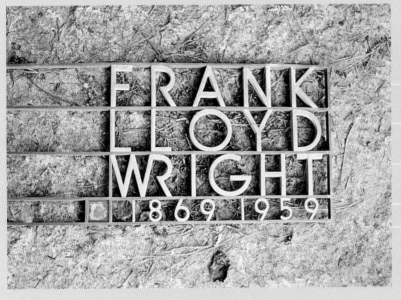

**Notes**
1. F Gutheim (ed), *Frank Lloyd Wright on Architecture*, Grosset & Dunlap (New York), 1941, p136.
2. Brendan Gill, *Many Masks*, Heinemann (London), 1988. Gill first introduces his notion of Wright's masks on p 9.
3. Frank Lloyd Wright, *An Autobiography*, Horizon Press (New York), third edition, 1977, p 163.
4. Frank Lloyd Wright, *The Future of Architecture*, Meridian (New York), 1953, p 29 (transcript of a telecast on NBC, 17 May 1953).
5. Also known as the White Slave Traffic Act, it was passed in 1910 to create stiff penalties for the interstate transportation of women for immoral purposes. Aimed primarily to protect young women from prostitution, its terms also applied to cohabitation.
6. Ling Po, Taliesin Fellow, in conversation with the author, 1992.
7. F Gutheim (ed), *op cit*, p 136.
8. Gill, op cit, p 444.
9. Frank Lloyd Wright, *An Autobiography*, pp 541–2
10. Ibid, p.105.
11. Patrick Meehan, *The Master Architect*, Wiley (New York), 1984, p177.
12. John Lloyd Wright, *My Father Who Is on Earth*, Putnams (New York), 1946.
13. Originally founded in 1929 as a way for Wright to escape his creditors by selling shares in himself. Its main enterprises was the establishment of a 'School of Architecture' run on an apprenticeship basis at Wright's studio in Taliesin, Wisconsin. In practice they carried out large amounts of domestic, farm and building

'them asses' as an improvement on 'the masses'. The title he gave to his book on *lieber meister* Louis Sullivan (dead, so no longer a potential rival) was *Genius and the Mobocracy*,[20] a phrase which he might surely have thought applied to himself even more than to his former employer.

His methods with clients were less direct since he was immediately dependent on them to realise his designs, and they seemed to have their own ideas, a reluctance to part with their money and appaling furniture (in his eyes). The great individualist-artist's houses, despite his claim that they were portraits of his clients, were in fact based on a logic that, as Sir Herbert Read pointed out, 'implies that every house that Mr Wright built is his own house and the people who live in them are not his clients but his guests'.[21]

The masks Wright adopted were so many and so various that there hardly seems to have been anything else to him. Yet they were all, finally, in the service of his architecture. Wright was honest, if in nothing else, in his belief in the value of architecture and, of course, in the value of his own architecture. In a sense, his vision was him. It started before he was born when his mother gazed at engravings of French cathedrals. She later put them round his cot and in his nursery to stage-manage a genius for architecture.

Wright defended himself only on the comparatively few occasions when he felt this had become absolutely necessary, and at these times he gave away something of his inner self or, as I have come to feel, his lack of an inner self. He fell back on such phrases as, 'Well, that's how I am', 'I had to make a noise in the

world in order to get as much of the world's attention as I could'.[22] 'Be yourself', he would say followed by, 'I guess that's how I am.' His use of the third person 'he' when talking about himself in his autobiography can be seen as an attempt to pre-empt such situations – a kind of getting his retaliation in first. More illuminating are remarks he made at times when he was in extreme difficulty, when he seems to come near to baring his soul even to himself. He came up with: 'I guess my talent has severed me from myself all along', 'Character is fate and mine got me into heavy going' and 'I think I am too many people ever to put into one presentment'.[23]

Too many people or not a real person at all? Wright certainly believed in destiny and fate, which seems strangely at odds with his ideas on freedom and choice. His many masks can be peeled away but, like Peer Gynt's onion, what is left?

Wright was fearless and an indefatigable fighter. Despite all his many setbacks, illnesses and tribulations he never wavered in his determination to see his architecture built. His whole life was based on a strategy (philosophy is not a suitable word here, still less morality) grounded in means and ends. This legitimised, in his own eyes, virtually any words or actions that would further the creation of his vision for architecture (and therefore his vision for the life of people in society). Of course, this is open to the objections that other approaches to life that have a similar methodology attract. One thinks of utilitarianism and its justification for the punishment of innocent people, or of religious persecution or political spin and vote rigging. Apart from anything else, the arguments put forward for such approaches are simplistic, logically unsound and ethically naive. Nevertheless, they are at the core of many beliefs and attract much support, so here Wright – no doubt much to his chagrin if he had

work as well as acting as free
architectural assistants, all the
time having to pay substantial
fees for the privilege.
14. John Lloyd Wright, *op cit*,
p 68.
15. Wright also used the title
'Broadacre City: a new
community plan' for an article
in *Architectural Record* in
April 1935.
16. In the context of Wright's
self-confessed Platonism (not
a guarantee that he had even
read Plato) it is interesting to
consider Socrates' analysis of
love in the *Symposium*, into an
ascending hierarchy, in
modern terms, of sex, fame
and art. As we shall see, this
is very close to Wright's own
position.
17. Frank Lloyd Wright, *A
Testament*, Bramhall House
(New York), 1957, p 58. It is the
name of a section in Part 1.
18. Frank Lloyd Wright, *An
Autobiography*, p 555.
19. For example, ibid, p 653.
20. Frank Lloyd Wright, *Genius
and the Mobocracy*, Secker &
Warburg (London), first
English edition, 1972.
21. Meryle Secrest, *Frank
Lloyd Wright*, Chatto & Windus
(London), 1992, p 553.
22. Gill, *op cit*, p 489.
23. Secrest, *op cit*, p 377.
24. Gill, *op cit*, pp 491–2.
25. Russian-born Ayn Rand
espoused an extreme form of
Nietzschean morality based on
rational self-interest and
unrestrained capitalism.
26. Gill, *op cit*, p 478.

realised this – is nearer to the collectivism he despised than to the free spirit he espoused.

Most of Wright's accoutrements were adopted deliberately, others perhaps came from a more subconscious spring. In the first category one might place his dwellings, his motor cars, his clothes, his care with photographic images (of himself, of course, but even more so of his buildings), the Taliesin Fellowship, his employment of skilled renders (from Marion Mahoney at the Oak Park studio in Chicago before the First World War right up to Ling Po after the Second World War), the low chairs his visitors and clients were obliged to sit on when they were in his company, and the fact that he never visited clients in their own homes but insisted that they came to his (or to the Plaza suite in New York which he had remodelled for himself). In the second, perhaps, was his habit of seeking out horizontal surfaces and swinging his legs up and down while talking (he seemed larger) or his predilection for cantilever hats (acquired from Olgivanna).

Fame for Wright must have seemed necessary. If you knew that you were the greatest architect in the world, how could you tolerate the fame of others whom you knew to be inferior? When he first read *The Fountainhead*, as four million other Americans would do, he was impressed. Its central character was an individual with his own determination. He liked the basically Nietzschean radical philosophy, but when he met the author, Ayn Rand (after she had sent him the first three chapters), he objected to the architect being red-headed and tall, and to the name Roark. He finally disapproved of the ending, saying it was absurd that the architect,

Howard Roark, would destroy his own building. Wright declared that he himself would never have allowed it to be built other than in complete accordance with his own plans.[24] That is certainly true, but he had assumed that the book could only be about him. This was not entirely the case: Ayn Rand had a philosophical mission[25] and, as a novelist, produced several vehicles to broadcast her thesis. Although Wright designed a very grand house for her, which she liked but could not afford ('Write more then', he had said when she produced this excuse), she finally bought one designed by his erstwhile apprentice Richard Neutra. Wright disliked the film of the book partly because Gary Cooper was more famous than himself!

Wright was more worshipped than admired and more denigrated than worshipped. When Marilyn Monroe was a client her husband at the time, the playwright Arthur Miller, commented that Wright reminded him of WC Fields,[26] a harsh but plausible comparison. But his architecture was both admired and universally eulogised. This is how he would have wanted it; he only sought fame for the sake of his architecture. Like Wagner and his music before him – the composer was an equally reprehensible and ruthless reprobate, with a wife curiously akin to Olgivanna in her guardianship of the Master's reputation and role as high priestess of the cult after his death – Wright was convinced that his architecture, once produced, could stand on its own and would ensure its own eternal fame. All his behaviour outside architecture tells us nothing about his inner personality – he existed only as a manifestation of his work. It was a means to an end – as he was. ⌂

Howard Martin has most recently been Director of Undergraduate Studies at the School of Architecture and Landscape at Kingston University, Surrey, where he has also been the principal lecturer in architectural history and leader of the diploma course. He studied architecture at the Bartlett (UCL) and has masters degrees in philosophy from Cambridge University and history from London University.

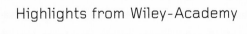

# The Church of Santa Maria in Marco de Canavezes

Designing places of worship in the 21st century relies on a careful definition of their use. When Alvaro Siza designed a Catholic church outside Oporto in Portugal, he found that the changes in liturgy brought about by Vatican II in 1962 meant that he was unable to resort to traditional models of church design. Reconsidered in every aspect, Santa Maria in Marco de Canavezes is hewn out of Siza's personal experience as well as his much favoured Functionalist approach.

Opposite
On a granite base, the pristine white 30 x 16.5 metre form of the church will create one side of a small civic space, an *adro*, with the priest's house and a parish centre. Two projections flank the main west door, which is used on ceremonial occasions: the left-hand one is the baptistery, 5 x 6 metres on plan and 7 metres high; on the right is the bell tower. Even though the bell's peals are controlled by computer from the sacristy, these elements 'make the church, seem a church', but use a modernist formal language.

Below
Site plan. The church lies on a sloping site, its precinct bounded by a road, an old people's home and some private houses. The parish centre comprises a Sunday School and auditorium on the south side of the adro, facing north to the church, and a priest's house which completes the adro to the northwest of the church. The volumes relate to each other, with the lesser buildings mediating between the church and the landscape.

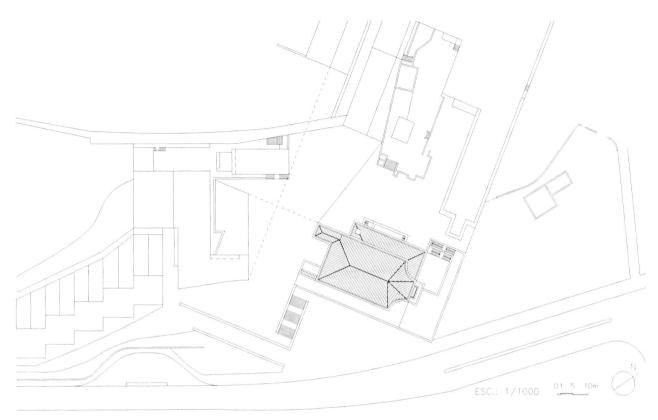

ESC.: 1/1000    01 5 10m

PLANTA DE IMPLANTAÇÃO

Alvaro Siza describes himself as a Functionalist architect so, when he was designing the Church of Santa Maria in Marco de Canavezes outside his home town of Oporto in northern Portugal, he 'looked to the functions inside a church'. As a boy, he knew these functions intimately. 'I had a Catholic education, as in my time all Portuguese people did ... the boys would go [to church] with their mothers.' But as they grew up, 'We would begin to go outside, as the men did, to say some jokes and to smoke a cigarette. The cigarette breaks became longer and one day we stopped going to church.'

As a result, when a young priest – who had some architecture student friends who went to work for Siza – asked him to design a church, 'the hierarchy was not so happy ... The bishop said "He is not Catholic" but the priest insisted'. This insistence led to 'a very difficult and complex work'; partly because Siza had to come to terms with the significant changes in church rituals since he had attended regularly, perhaps more because he had to use purely architectural sensibilities to make the building operate as, and look like, a church. Convention and clichés would not do. 'I didn't want to make the cross a solution for the design,' he explains.

'One building,' he continues, 'can touch on many aspects of architecture. It talks about the problems of architecture today.' His design is an attempt, as a Functionalist, to make some architectural sense of the liturgy as it is after the Second

Vatican Council, in particular the practice of the priest facing the congregation rather than the apse. This makes the apse, 'the big area behind the altar with sculpture and paintings to which the priest looked', which is the glory of so much Catholic architecture, 'become rather strange'. The strong heritage of great church architecture is a 'kind of inhibition ... almost unuseful for the problems of today.'

Siza explains that, faced with this dilemma, many architects started to base their designs on auditoriums, and 'it went well'. But, 'for some people, including me, something is missing.' That something draws on childhood memories: 'The impression of mystery, dense atmosphere, sometimes of darkness, some elements in space we could not understand.' And then the loss of that mystery to the temptations of tobacco, just as the Church itself pulled away from mystery in its urge to seem 'relevant'. So personal subjectivity interweaves with objective Functionalism. Siza's accumulated skill, gathered through 50 years in architecture rather than the experience of regular attendance at church ceremonies, becomes the means to recreate the mysteries of faith.

It's the sort of psychological raw material from which Graham Greene fashioned novels with no discernible

Below top
The inclined, curving wall with its high windows, and the convex shapes, lend the interior a dynamic quality which makes a perfect setting for the drama of celebrating Mass, or for slower and more personal contemplation of the changing light as the sun's rays flow around the space. The asymmetrically placed cross intensifies the mysterious dynamic: Siza considered a formal, axial placing before remembering Ronchamp. The space is never finite or still. It always hints at something beyond its limits, yet it achieves this by purely architectural means – shape, light, colour, material, space and texture – rather than overt symbols.

Below bottom left
Cross section through the church, looking towards the altar. The inclined north wall conceals high windows, allowing light from an untracable source to permeate the space. To the side are the sacristy and confessional spaces, with the funeral chapel below.

Below bottom right
Cross section looking towards the west door. The font is visible in the baptistry.

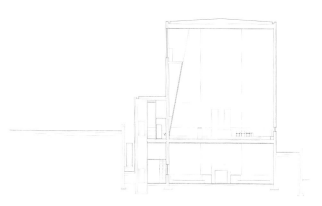
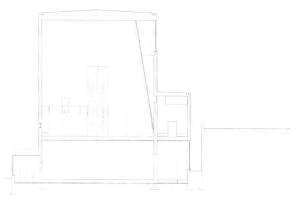

Below left
Long section looking south. At eye level there is a long, low horizontal window which perhaps relieves boredom enough to stop the men leaving for extended cigarette breaks, and reminds the priest of an obligation to the greater community not just the regular attenders at church.

Below right
Long section looking north. Beyond the cross is the way to the sacristy, but the priest enters through the door in the wall and passes through the congregation to the altar. This requirement, a demand of the theological advisers, helped to solve a practical problem: the door marks the point where the wood dado stops and becomes marble, which is needed in the baptistery because of the presence of water. Below the altar is the funeral chapel, with a small courtyard where mourners can gather, 'to discuss business and tell the latest jokes'.

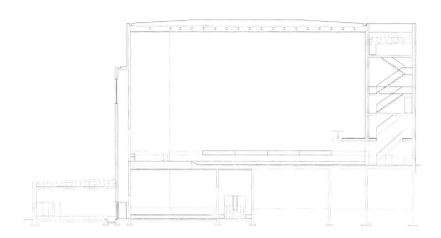

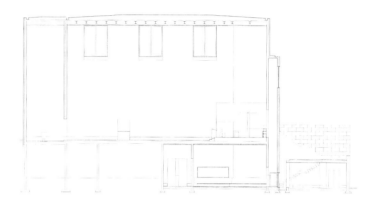

effort. As an architect, Siza can be economical with the physical raw material – 'There are very few materials', he says, 'marble, wood, plaster, ceramics, outside plaster and granite' – but still achieve spaces of richness and complexity. With great discipline in detail so that each junction reinforces an overall idea, light, shade and views become part of the palette. At times the space is warm and welcoming, at others cold, austere and contemplative; the movement of the sun during the day and through the seasons becomes one of the cycles of change in the building. Siza is aware of the theatrical aspects of ritual, and the movement of the celebrants and congregation during the Mass is an entirely human pattern; but the human pattern of the Church calendar, of feast and holy days, interacts with nature. The giant west door, 10 metres high and 3 metres wide, opens on such special occasions: the dazzling crack of sunlight might put some people in mind of the opening of the tomb. Here the natural and artificial meld together in the manner of all great religious architecture.

The church's outer form is deceptively simple. Using the sloping site gave access at two levels. The lower is a small funeral chapel; above rises the pristine white church. At the west end two short wings, one the baptistery and the other the bell tower, project forward to form a small enclosure in front of the ceremonial door. A pair of curves at the eastern end, concave on the outside and convex inside, reverse the traditional form of the apse; Siza enjoys a friend's rationalisation that this shape tends to push the priest towards the congregation, in the spirit of Vatican II. These devices achieve his aim of wanting to 'make the church look like church' even if the urban composition, with a priest's residence and parish centre flanking the church to form a piazza, is not complete, and despite Siza's 'panic' on seeing the site for the first time. 'When a town offers a site for making something,' he reflects, 'this site is often the worst the town has.' It was 'a half-ruined landscape', on the line of a former national road which is now included in the urban area. There was one significant building in the vicinity, an old people's home, whose 'straight volume and dimension' made something solid to which the church and associated buildings could respond.

Inside, the pristine and sunlight-etched forms soften and become more fluid. Siza cites Ronchamp and Aalto churches as being among the few distinguished modernist ones; with its high windows, subtle forms including an inwardly sloping and curved north wall, and off-centre cross, the references in his building are discernible. But there are other influences. Siza had to address the apparently contradictory requirements of theological experts: one wanted the baptistery near the

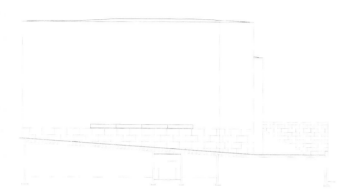

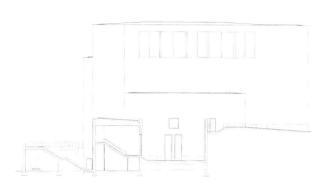

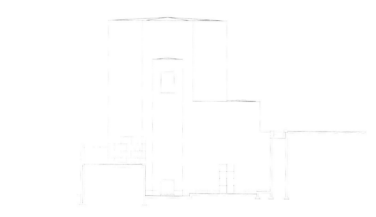

altar so that all the congregation to see the ceremony;
another claimed that someone should first be received
into the Church through baptism before entering the
sacred space. This, the solution that was adopted, does
not follow the strict letter of the new post-Vatican-II
liturgy. 'It's the new, new liturgy,' Siza replies.

In striving towards a new, new liturgy Siza's personal
memories, perceptions and intuitions intertwine with
theology to assume a greater significance. There are
wonderful practical and sympathetic touches: a space
for people to leave the funeral chapel and 'have a
cigarette and tell new jokes'; a hole in the massive
marble altar where the priest can place his feet. Even
ordained priests are human. And a low, horizontal
window gives the celebrant a view across the
congregation and out towards the town, making sense
of facing the people. Siza himself, perhaps harking back
to an adolescent wish to be a sculptor, made the cross
of two pieces of wood and gold leaf – an attempt to
include a figure of Christ was 'a disaster' – and decided
on its asymmetrical placing. It was his memory of a
church in Palermo, Sicily, where a mosaic of Christ
Pantocrator shimmers in the apse, that helped to
resolve the character of the apse. There was no chance
of a mosaic, in any case – an Orthodox form of
decoration – but Siza's cross helped to clarify the
manipulation of light at the end of a sunny day, when 'a
wonderful golden light approaches the altar'. ⌂

# SHoP/Sharples Holden Pasquarelli

Buildability remains a special problem for avant-garde architects who design almost exclusively using computers. Budget overruns and materials compromises help to highlight friction between the limitless possibilities available in virtual reality and the limitations of construction in the real world. At stake is the very emergence of the new computer-generated amorphous aesthetic. Here, Craig Kellogg looks at the work of SHoP/Sharples Holden Pasquarelli, a no-nonsense digital practice in Manhattan that embraces constraints at every stage of design. Tempered with a healthy dose of reality, the firm seeks to realise the warped forms currently in vogue — but to build them with less than the usual fuss.

SHoP/Sharples Holden Pasquarelli

Top
This little jewellery shop, Me & Ro, in Elizabeth Street, Manhattan, was completed by ShoP in November 1999. Passers-by are drawn in to the boutique by a lily pond in the shop window.

Above
SHoP/Sharples Holden Pasquarelli (left to right): William W Sharples, Coren D Sharples, Christopher R Sharples, Gregg A Pasquarelli and Kimberly J Holden.

**Mitchell Park, Greenport, New York.** Phase one (the new steel-and-glass carousel house, amphitheatre and harbour walk) was completed in June 2001. Mitchell Park is a $9 million public amenity currently being constructed on five waterfront acres in the village of Greenport. To begin work, the architects digitally mapped outside forces that would tug at their scheme, noting a nearby train station, existing commercial wharves, adjacent retail structures and a ferry terminal to the west. The plan that evolved enhances flow, directing pedestrian traffic along paths of least resistance across what was once an open field. In addition to a harbour walk that skirts the water's edge, attractions will include a dockmaster's house, the amphitheatre and the carousel house. Lending some consistency to the architecture, throughout the park the designers have emphasised a natural palette of steel, etched glass, bluestone pavers, weathered natural hardwoods and lead-coated copper roofing.

Below left
The completed carousel in Mitchell Park.

Below right
Blended fronts diagram of Mitchell Park.

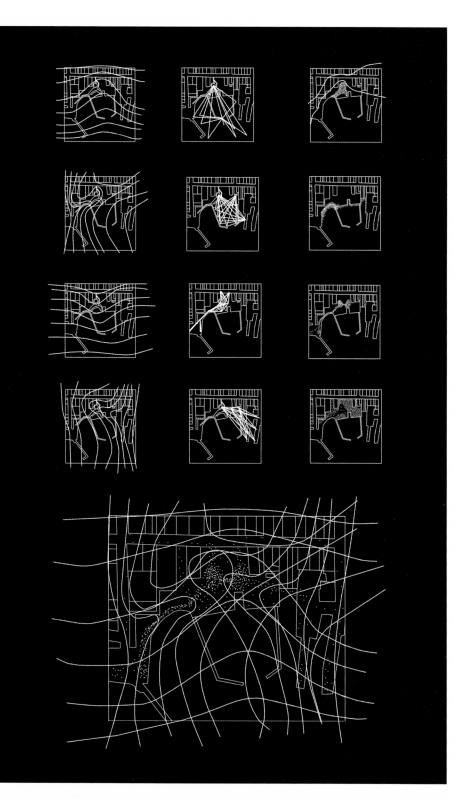

The partners of SHoP/Sharples Holden Pasquarelli work at the low-rent end of East 37th Street, in a ratty, unfashionable Manhattan neighbourhood on the fringes of Midtown. Their modest office loft, which they renovated themselves, is clean and quiet, with a computer at every station. First impressions suggest a hungry young firm with just a few clever things built. The partners have, in fact, realised only a small number of designs since SHoP was founded in 1997. Major completed works include a portable trade-show booth, an experimental outdoor installation and a waterfront park with a carousel house, amphitheatre and harbour walk. Manhattan retail stores were also designed and built for two downtown fashion boutiques: an all-black box with high-contrast lighting for the clothier Costume National, and a funkier, compact shop with a lily pond in the showcase window for a jeweller called Me & Ro. Nevertheless, important major commissions either under way or in the planning stages suggest SHoP is already a fierce competitor among Manhattan architects.

Bill, Chris and Coren Sharples joined forces with Kimberly Holden and Gregg Pasquarelli in 1997. The five clicked almost immediately. All had attended graduate school in architecture at Columbia University and were working under contract to others. But occasionally the partners would drop their apprenticeships to prepare entries to open architectural competitions. 'We approached it as a job,' Coren Sharples explains. 'This wasn't a hobby for us. When the time was needed and a goal had to be reached, there was only one way … put in the time.'

Their early proposals – conceived to the last detail then drawn in ink by hand – began attracting awards. SHoP is one of the few American firms with a reputation built on its entries to open architectural competitions. With some regularity the firm has been short-listed and invited to prepare more concrete proposals. A third-place finish in a competition to design the new waterside park for the village of Greenport, New York, has evolved into a major commission. (Phase One was opened to the public in June 2001.)

The park plan for Greenport was developed digitally. Computer-mapping has allowed SHoP to begin formalising and digitising traditional architectural processes. Usually, hidden beneath layers of complexity, efficiencies are uncovered and opportunities found. Site surveys and community meetings produced a 'catalogue' of forces representing limitations and needs that would constrain the development of the park. To help analyse data using the computer, the partners collapsed the forces into a 'blended fronts diagram'. Forms, siting and shapes for programme features were generated directly as a result of the process.

Though the amorphous aesthetic popular among next-generation digital-architects can seem baroque, SHoP's squishy shapes often solve problems. Light Bridges at Jay Street is a pair of apartment towers proposed for Brooklyn, carefully plotted angles in plan change from floor to floor; as they ascend, the towers do appear to have melted slightly. But the fact that the angles change constantly has somehow permitted the partners to skirt zoning restrictions that would render their apartments illegal, since the towers would otherwise be considered to be unacceptably close together.

Studiously, the firm avoids 'aestheticising something that could impact the way architecture is produced'. Is it fair to judge the towers ugly? Are we simply unprepared for them? Chris Sharples draws a parallel with Frank Lloyd Wright's Guggenheim, a great unexpected spiral, like a spaceship landed incongruously among Manhattan's most expensive, conservative apartment blocks. 'Changing the way the deck is stacked, you can be intuitive without preconceiving,' he suggests. This frees architects to take new inspirations. A full accounting of limitations, needs and constraints, Sharples says, should steer architectural form and, ultimately, shape.

SHoP calls this process 'performance modelling,' a design strategy that is, frankly, more familiar to engineers than architects. It's 'how a building will perform,' Coren Sharples explains, 'an idea that can be manipulated – not a fixed formal vision.' Professors in school told her: 'You have to be strong. When you have an idea, you can't let anyone water it down. You can't give up, because people will nibble away at it and you'll have nothing left.' The SHoP philosophy, by contrast, is flexible. 'A really good idea,' Coren Sharples suggests, 'can be made to serve all the needs.'

Since performance models build flexibility into the process, expectations for a particular project can be held constant while the physical expression remains free to evolve. The SHoP proposal for the Museum of Sex has navigated a rocky road towards realisation, with additional bumps to come. The concept, however, remains easily summed up in a single word: skin. Because the design was originally created for a pair of founders who have since split, the site for the sex museum is now in question. Still, other forces and expectations for the facility remain in place. No matter where in Manhattan the museum might be built, space is likely to be expensive – and tight. So the new museum will, for instance, require the same sorts of multifunctional elements embedded (in the skin) that are included in the current proposal.

While digital-architects have argued that the introduction of computers should begin to alter design conventions from the predigital age, SHoP takes the

Below
In ShoP's scheme for a pair of apartment towers in Brooklyn – Light Bridges at Jay Street –
angles were carefully plotted in plan so as to change from floor to floor. This permitted the
partners to skirt zoning restrictions in a characteristically pragmatic manner so that the
towers weren't considered to be unacceptably close together.

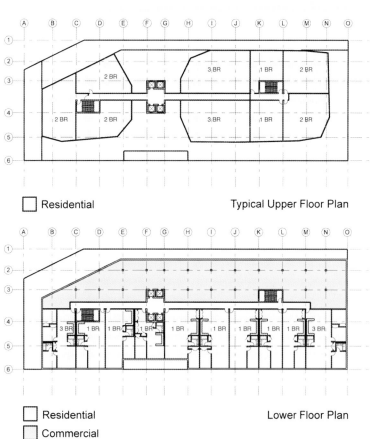

Residential                                           Typical Upper Floor Plan

Residential                                           Lower Floor Plan
Commercial

Computer-generated forms were fabricated on site by apprentices. Rather like
a wave, the principal wood structure crested over a series of dressing-room stalls
where street clothes could be changed for beachwear. Overhead, circulating
water ran down the roof and into a one of several very shallow pools edged by
a wood-slat deck. Elsewhere on the same site, smaller platforms and booths
continued the amorphous aesthetic, while a cluster of plumbed poles spritzed
an adjoining area christened the 'mist garden'.

computer one step further, into the construction
process. The undulating trade-show booth SHoP
designed on the computer for the US magazine
*Architecture* was assembled using custom-cut shingles
of titanium. The most efficient solution required
triangular modules of various sizes, though variations
in size would seem to add complexity. Computers
helped to bridge the gap. Digitally, the architects nested
the range of modules on to sheet layouts to minimise
the titanium that would be wasted as scrap. Layout
drawings were emailed to a fabricator who laser-cut
pieces, simultaneously etching each with a number
that corresponded to its placement on the surface of
the display. On the convention floor, what might have
been extremely complicated and expensive to erect was
then quickly and easily built by numbers. 'If we do not
effect the manufacturing process,' Chris Sharples says,
'it affects time, cost and creativity.'

## Office statement
Rather than focusing upon a vocabulary of pliant
and reconfigurable forms, our office is researching
a procedural agenda, or practice, that is pliant
and reconfigurable. We believe that constructs of

Below
Museum of Sex, Manhattan, New York. Though it remains stalled at an early stage of development due to fund-raising shortfalls, this mid-rise museum concept served to establish a public profile for SHoP. In the current scheme, the proposed midtown Manhattan site for the sex expo is an L-shaped corner lot on Fifth Avenue with views to the thrusting Empire State Building spire beyond. Since the lot is narrow, with two highly visible street facades, the flamboyant layered skin of the 40,000-square-foot building functions variously to filter daylight, accommodate displays and allow vertical movement. Placement and curvature of walls plays to the needs of functions within. The innermost layer conceals infrastructure within a continuous sculptural shape. Above the ground floor, the outer facade comprises a glass-and-steel veil that thickens, curves and peels apart. At street level, however, large transparent windows would deny sexuality its usual taboo, 'inviting entry with nothing to hide'.

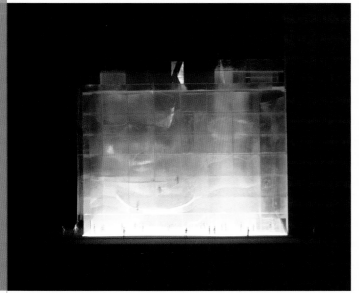

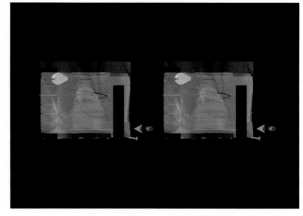

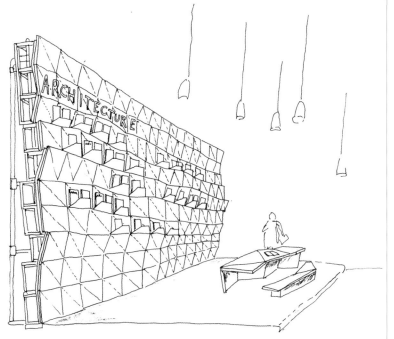

architecture respond, by degrees, to the influence of forces present in the environment. Our research on the generation of space and form has led to the development of systems that can be configured to address and respond to the variable influences of context. Here, a new definition of context must be used: the confluence of financial, physical, social, temporal, and legislative influences that prepare a thickened membrane within which an architectural intrusion can be inserted. Each project attempts to develop a methodology of insertion and to create a conceptual engine supple enough to respond and react to external forces while maintaining the project's integrity, spatiality and coherence.

These provisional typologies do not represent nor reflect a formal condition that can be equated with a single origin or physical contextual source, but rather are surrounding fields. The development of a design intent into a field of play allows the responsive typological system to search for the dissolution of boundaries and generate a network of ambient unities that are both singular and continuous. The result should not be viewed as the implementation of smoothed difference, but rather as providing a comprehensive and ambient blending of events and context on to implied multivalent arrays, protean trajectories and labile forms.

The office believes that this discourse can only be understood through actual construction, using both spatial and nonspatial agendas to reach the point of translation between conceptual and physical solutions. Our office uses a mixture of three-dimensional computer form generation techniques along with rapid prototyping, model building and architectural detailing in our own woodshop to provide a spatial solution that is open, gestural, revealing, precise and unique for each of our clients. ⋳

## Resumé

1990    Christopher Sharples obtained his Master of Architecture degree from Columbia University. Following his graduation, Chris spent 2 1/2 years living and working in Japan.

1994    William Sharples, Coren Sharples, Kimberly Holden and Gregg Pasquarelli obtained Master of Architecture degrees from Columbia University.

1996    Chris, Bill and Coren Sharples received the commission for Mitchell Park, a waterfront revitalisation project, in Greenport, New York after placement in an International Design Competition.

1997    Chris, Bill and Coren Sharples, Kimberly Holden and Gregg Pasquarelli received Honorable Mention for their entry for the Sunshelter Competition sponsored by the Van Alen Institute and the Hudson Park Conservancy. The Sharpleses joined with Holden and Pasquarelli on the design of the Costume National store in SoHo, New York. SHoP/Sharples Holden Pasquarelli was formed in late 1997.

1998    SHoP received a Lumen Award from the Illuminating Engineering Society of North America for Costume National. The design for the Museum of Sex was commissioned.

1999    The groundbreaking for the Mitchell Park occurred in January. SHoP received a P/A (Progressive Architecture) Award Citation for the design of the Museum of Sex in Manhattan. Me & Ro, a jewelry store in Manhattan, was completed.

2000    The firm won first place in the Young Architect's Program Competition jointly sponsored by the Museum of Modern Art and P.S.1 Contemporary Arts Center. The winning scheme, entitled Dunescape, was completed in June 2000. SHoP received the commissions for a mid-rise apartment tower in Brooklyn, New York and for the new School of the Arts for Columbia University.

2001    SHoP received the 2001 Emerging Voices Award from the Architectural League of New York and the 2001 Academy Award in Architecture from the American Academy of Arts and Letters. The construction of Phase One of Mitchell Park in Greenport, New York was completed. The gallery/ showroom for Dakota Jackson was completed in Soho, New York. The firm received commissions for the Rubell Family Collection Gallery in Miami, Florida and the Brooklyn Baseball Museum in Coney Island, New York.

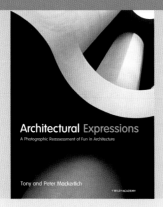

## ARCHITECTURAL EXPRESSIONS: A PHOTOGRAPHIC REASSESSMENT OF FUN IN ARCHITECTURE
Tony and Peter Mackertich

PB 0 471 49667 7; £19.99; 290 x 220 mm; 128 pages; October 2001

## ARCHITECTURE A–Z: A ROUGH GUIDE
Louis Hellman

PB 0 471 48957 3; £19.99; 290 x 220 mm; 184 pages; October 2001

Everyone values a sense of humour. Yet although architecture is undeniably the field of creative design which has the greatest impact on all of us, humour has long been a taboo subject within it. The Wiley-Academy books featured this month prove that – contrary to general perception, at least until recent times – humour does have a place in architecture.

Intent on making their mark, architects have often been inclined to focus so much on theoretical issues that they have alienated the man in the street. In particular, the high ideals of Modernism – intended to be a more democratic form of architecture, and at its best an honourable ethos leading to beautiful, clean designs – have sadly resulted in unsympathetic structures stripped bare of the embellishments that could engage the resident or passer-by. In recent years, however, attitudes have begun to change. Architects are gradually becoming willing to acknowledge that humour need not be banished in order for architecture to progress. Buildings have started to appear that combine practicality, artistic integrity and cutting-edge technology with a dash of wit.

As advocates of this change, photographer Peter Mackertich and his brother, art director Tony Mackertich, have spent a considerable amount of time over the last 30 years travelling the world and making a photographic record of buildings with a sense of fun. *Architectural Expressions* presents some 140 of their stunning photographs, boldly juxtaposing 'high' architecture with more lowly structures.

From the exuberance of the Michelin Building in London and the otherworldiness of the Einstein Tower in Potsdam at the beginning of the 20th century, the journey proceeds through the kitsch Egyptomania of the 1920s and the light-hearted 1930s obsession with ship and automobile forms. The Mackertichs then go on to feature the brash roadside structures of Los Angeles that kept the flame burning in the otherwise deadpan mid-century, with doughnut and hotdog sellers housed in giant representations of their products, and 'Big Men' perched atop showrooms holding aloft their wares. The late 1970s and 1980s saw a turning point in architecture with a lighter spirit creeping in, represented here through

projects by Philip Johnson, SITE, Frank Gehry, John Outram and Eric Owen Moss. Finally, in the last few years, the full potential of combining the latest structural possibilities with a sense of playfulness has been realised with projects such as Future Systems' Lord's Media Centre and Will Alsop's Peckham Library in London, and Frank Gehry's Guggenheim Museum in Bilbao. This book, with its lavish full-colour photography, quirky captions and short explanatory texts, proves the point that architecture need not be deadly serious to be valid.

From humour in architecture to humorous comment on architecture. Louis Hellman, dubbed 'Architecture's official satirist since the 1960s' by the *Guardian*, has established an international reputation for his cartoons on architectural themes. Best known for his 'archi-têtes' – portraits of celebrated architects using forms derived from the style and components of their buildings – he is blessed with a rare ability to be amusing and educative at the same time.

His latest work, *Architecture A–Z*, offers an engaging introduction to the world of architecture by way of the alphabet. Each letter has an entry covering a particular topic, not only examining architecture itself but also setting it in a broader social, political and cultural context. From 'Architecture' to 'Zoo' by way of 'Energy', 'Gothic', 'Machine Age' and 'Women', the brilliantly perceptive cartoons and brief texts illustrating each subject are as entertaining for the architectural ingénue as they are for the established professional in the field. Combining the wit and insight of the cartoonist with the architect's inside knowledge of the profession, the drawings are both amusing and thought-provoking.

Both books provide a little light relief in a field that often takes itself too seriously, and either would be an ideal Christmas gift for anyone interested or involved in architecture. ↶ *Abigail Grater*

*HIS INVENTION SO FERTILE: A Life of Christopher Wren* by Adrian Tinniswood, Jonathan Cape (London), 2001, HB £25

Adrian Tinniswood 's particular biographical interest in Wren lies in the 'circuitous path that he took to become Britain's most eminent architect'. Before designing his first building at the age of 31, Sir Christopher Wren held two prestigious academic posts: first as Professor of Astronomy at Gresham College, London, and then as the Savilian Professor of Astronomy at Oxford. Wren's scientific enquiries did not, however, stop at the stars – a point that Tinniswood dramatically makes in his introduction through a detailed description of Wren, as a young don at Oxford, performing a canine splectonomy. (The object of this operation, which involved removing a spaniel's spleen to see whether it could survive without it, was to disprove the Roman medical notion of the four humours – melancholy being the humour secreted by the spleen.) Before devoting himself professionally to architecture on his appointment as Surveyor-General of King's Works in 1669, Wren's preoccupations within the mechanical sciences were catholic enough to be characterised by his biographer as restless. This 'restlessness' can be summed up by his activities during the 1660s for the Royal Society. Between February and June of 1667 alone, he is documented to have reported on the following at its weekly gatherings: a new kind of oil lamp that he had developed; a new level for measuring the horizon; curious hailstones shaped like marigolds, which he presented drawings of; the way grain stores worked in Danzig and in Russia; and his observations of how long flies can live after they have been decapitated.

Tinniswood's extremely thorough exploration of Wren's intellectual pursuits outside of architecture are interwoven with detailed research into the Wren family's social and political background. (His father and uncle were high-ranking Anglican clerics during the reign of Charles I, putting him at an advantage during the Restoration.) This all combines to give a rare account of the status of the architect in 17th-century England. The obvious interest in the events that brought Wren to hold such an auspicious place in architectural history, however, is never at the expense of descriptions of his architecture or its development. Tinniswood succeeds in providing, in a way that is remarkable given the limitations of a biography format, black-and-white visual references for buildings wherever they are necessary. Whereas photographs are confined to three plate sections, line drawings of plans are inserted in the text. This allows him to fully illustrate, for instance, the early design variations of St Paul's and Wren's 'exultation in the opportunity to experiment' with his City churches after the Great Fire of London by demonstrating their variety through their plans.

Whereas biography as a genre tends to attract a greater readership than architectural books, through its natural affinities with personality and the personal, this is certainly not the case with Tinniswood's book. Bar the bare facts – dates of births and deaths – little is known of Wren's conjugal or familial relationships. Rather than compensating with speculation, Tinniswood settles with what is documented and a well-qualified conviction 'that Wren's work was his life'. (As King's Commissioner for Rebuilding of London Churches after the Great Fire and Surveyor-General for nearly 50 years, he was responsible for not only a prodigious output in terms of the buildings that he oversaw as well as those he designed, but also an enormous amount of administration.) The moments that we come closest to Wren, the man, are during the chapter devoted to Wren's trip to Paris in 1665 when he met Bernini, and the passages where Tinniswood uses the diaries of Robert Hooke, Wren's closest companion and colleague, to provide a full picture of their shared social life. The book includes a remarkable account of the exact coffee houses where Hooke and Wren conversed and exchanged business. Putting the biographical genre to his own use, Tinniswood runs with his subject, spanning a vast expanse of time from the Civil War to the Georgians (Wren was 91 when he died) and intriguing his readers with a vast range of historical knowledge. ⬗ *Helen Castle*

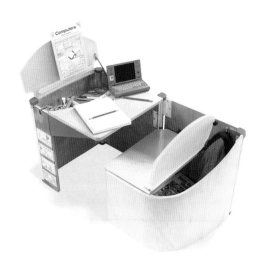

This article in the Site Lines series departs from its regular format of concentrating on individual buildings by featuring a school desk designed by New York architects Gans & Jelacic. Deborah Gans describes how this structure, shaped by New York City schoolchildren's needs, evolved into a flexible box that provides each student with a 'nomadic home base'.

Workbox is a combination desk, chair and locker. It is a cube that folds out to become a small enclosure complete with a coat hook, a piece of furniture whose surfaces can be personalised by its occupant, and a desk top with a cache for a computer. In these combinations, it belongs to the emerging genre of industrial design products that stress multifunctioning and adaptability. We discovered a real need for these qualities in our study of the New York public school system. As a consequence of placing in two competitions held by the School Construction Authority of New York (SCA), we received the commission to develop the 'next generation of school desk'. Over a period of two years, we worked directly with the manufacturing and sales divisions of a children's school supplies company and the SCA on aspects of material, assembly, form and function. The complexity of the demands on this Workbox helped to focus its design and broaden its market to the degree that it received a patent.

While the initial mandate from the SCA for a 'desk of the future' was technological, centred on the excitement of the computer, a web of social and cognitive needs emerged as we observed the school system with the desk in mind. The NYC school system is very overcrowded at this time. Hallways, closets, cafeterias and gymnasiums become classrooms on a shifting basis during the course of the day. Within the standard classroom as many as 30 children negotiate for room and attention. Many of them come from homes deprived

of privacy and space among many other things. The students needed not just desks; they needed a proprietary space within the school.

The environment of the classroom is in upheaval given the competing demands for traditional skills measured through standardised testing, mastery of new technologies, individual achievement and intensive socialisation. The classroom is now the setting in which children acquire a range of skills and habits – such as personal hygiene – usually associated with domestic and extracurricular settings. There is also need for continuity between school and the children's plugged-in, tech-savvy daily life. The new desk had to accommodate simultaneous tools of traditional and computer learning, and the concomitant multiple sets of cognitive and social processes. The desk had to foster real interaction as well as virtual experience.

Expanding on our observational brief, we incorporated oversized work, seating and storage areas into a piece whose overall dimensions meet the standards required by existing classrooms. The computer compartment lid opens without disturbing half of the desk top. When open, the lid functions as a writing surface and book ledge. There is a bookshelf under the seat and a coat hook behind it. Besides the pleasure associated with a room of one's own, this

individualised storage has public health advantages such as the control of head lice, etc.

The desk behaves as a kind of nomadic home base. It folds up, locks and moves while remaining identifiable. This mobility actually benefits the standard classroom as well as overcrowded schools because the desks can be clustered in many ways. We favour a pinwheel configuration in which children sit diagonally across from one another, a positioning that allows both some privacy and interaction over the open lid. The closed desk box serves as a table or platform (you can stand on it).

The design development took place in the context of the manufacturer's factory, where the precision required by furniture that moves in many directions had to be met with simple materials like wood, simple tools like jigsaws and simple processes like drilling. These factors led us to a material system that would preserve the flexibility and individuation we were after within the city's budget.

Almost like a building structure, the Workbox has an extruded aluminum frame and plywood panel system. The custom-made hinge and column and the stock plywood panels can be cut to any length and assembled 'dry' with standard tools and bolts. This allowed us to develop a series of ergonomically correct sizes without waste of material or change of manufacturing set-up. The panels can have a variety of finishes in any colour. Currently, they have a

blackboard and marker-board laminate, and a sealed birch veneer. There is a pocket for the student's name and photograph.

For its appealing qualities of colour and translucency, as well as for its material toughness and precise forming, we specified injected moulded plastic for the caps and lids. While the material itself is cheap, the forms are terribly expensive which led us to double up on the mould use. The top and bottom caps are made from a single form. The centre of the cap is removed at the bottom of the desk to receive ball-bearing castors that allow the desk to roll when unoccupied. Another mould can serve for both the seat back and desk top.

Workbox is currently in use in a public school in Staten Island, in a demanding situation where children with special physical and learning needs have a classroom half the standard width. We are developing a system of screens using the aluminium extrusions and panels that can line entire classrooms or define smaller spaces within. In response to constant enquiry we are also marketing the desk for home use. The child-as-client within the social construct of the public school system has given us a new way of viewing mass-produced objects. It turns out that these qualities are valued almost everywhere. ☠ *Deborah Gans*

# Subscribe Now for 2001

As an influential and prestigious architectural publication, *Architectural Design* has an almost unrivalled reputation worldwide. Published bi-monthly, it successfully combines the currency and topicality of a newsstand journal with the editorial rigour and design qualities of a book. Consistently at the forefront of cultural thought and design since the 60s, it has time and again proved provocative and inspirational – inspiring theoretical, creative and technological advances. Prominent in the 80s for the part it played in Post-Modernism and then in Deconstruction, ∆ has recently taken a pioneering role in the technological revolution of the 90s. With ground-breaking titles dealing with cyberspace and hypersurface architecture, it has pursued the conceptual and critical implications of high-end computer software and virtual realities. ∆

## ∆ Architectural Design

**SUBSCRIPTION RATES 2001**
Institutional Rate: UK £150
Personal Rate: UK £97
Discount Student* Rate: UK £70
OUTSIDE UK
Institutional Rate: US $225
Personal Rate: US $145
Student* Rate: US $105

*Proof of studentship will be required when placing an order. Prices reflect rates for a 2001 subscription and are subject to change without notice.

**TO SUBSCRIBE**
**Phone** your credit card order:
UK/Europe: +44 (0)1243 843 828
USA: +1 212 850 6645
**Fax** your credit card order to:
UK/Europe: +44 (0)1243 770 432
USA: +1 212 850 6021

**Email** your credit card order to:
cs-journals@wiley.co.uk
**Post** your credit card or cheque order to:

**UK/Europe:** John Wiley & Sons Ltd.
Journals Administration Department
1 Oldlands Way
Bognor Regis
West Sussex PO22 9SA
UK

**USA:** John Wiley & Sons Ltd.
Journals Administration Department
605 Third Avenue
New York, NY 10158
USA

Please include your postal delivery address with your order.

All ∆ volumes are available individually.
To place an order please write to:
John Wiley & Sons Ltd
Customer Services
1 Oldlands Way
Bognor Regis
West Sussex PO22 9SA

Please quote the ISBN number of the issue(s) you are ordering.

∆ is available to purchase on both a subscription basis and as individual volumes

○ I wish to subscribe to ∆ Architectural Design at the **Institutional rate of £150.**

○ I wish to subscribe to ∆ Architectural Design at the **Personal rate of £97.**

○ I wish to subscribe to ∆ Architectural Design at the **Student rate of £70.**

**STARTING FROM ISSUE 1/2001.**

○ Payment enclosed by Cheque/Money order/Drafts.

Value/Currency £/US$ _____

○ Please charge £/US$ _____ to my credit card.

Account number:

☐☐☐☐☐☐☐☐☐☐☐☐☐☐☐☐☐

Expiry date:

☐☐☐☐☐

Card: Visa/Amex/Mastercard/Eurocard *(delete as applicable)*

Cardholder's signature _____
Cardholder's name _____
Address _____
_____
_____ Post/Zip Code _____

Recepient's name _____
Address _____
_____
_____ Post/Zip Code _____

**I would like to buy the following Back Issues at £19.99 each:**

○ ∆ 153 Looking Back in Envy, Jan Kaplicky

○ ∆ 152 Green *Architecture*, Brian Edwards

○ ∆ 151 *New Babylonians*, Iain Borden + Sandy McCreery

○ ∆ 150 *Architecture + Animation*, Bob Fear

○ ∆ 149 *Young Blood*, Neil Spiller

○ ∆ 148 *Fashion and Architecture*, Martin Pawley

○ ∆ 147 *The Tragic in Architecture*, Richard Patterson

○ ∆ 146 *The Transformable House*, Jonathan Bell and Sally Godwin

○ ∆ 145 *Contemporary Processes in Architecture*, Ali Rahim

○ ∆ 144 *Space Architecture*, Dr Rachel Armstrong

○ ∆ 143 *Architecture and Film II*, Bob Fear

○ ∆ 142 *Millennium Architecture*, Maggie Toy and Charles Jencks

○ ∆ 141 *Hypersurface Architecture II*, Stephen Perrella

○ ∆ 140 *Architecture of the Borderlands*, Teddy Cruz

○ ∆ 139 *Minimal Architecture II*, Maggie Toy

○ ∆ 138 *Sci-Fi Architecture*, Maggie Toy

○ ∆ 137 *Des-Res Architecture*, Maggie Toy

○ ∆ 136 *Cyberspace Architecture II*, Neil Spiller

○ ∆ 135 *Ephemeral/Portable Architecture*, Robert Kronenburg